U0875576

暖小昕 / 编译

Living In My Favorite Way

用自己最爱的方式过一生

每天读一点暖心英文

北京联合出版公司
Beijing United Publishing Co.,Ltd.

图书在版编目（CIP）数据

用自己最爱的方式过一生 ： 汉英对照 / 暖小昕编译.
-- 北京 ： 北京联合出版公司，2015.4（2015.6重印）
（每天读一点暖心英文）
ISBN 978-7-5502-4904-2

Ⅰ. ①用… Ⅱ. ①暖… Ⅲ. ①英语－汉语－对照读物
②散文集－世界 Ⅳ. ①H319.4：Ⅰ

中国版本图书馆CIP数据核字（2015）第057412号

用自己最爱的方式过一生
编　　译：暖小昕
选题策划：王抗抗
责任编辑：李艳芬
封面设计：马顾本
版式设计：新兴工作室
责任校对：王　维

北京联合出版公司出版
（北京市西城区德外大街83号楼9层　100088）
小森（北京）印刷有限公司　新华书店经销
字数100千字　787毫米×1208毫米　1/32　6印张
2015年5月第1版　2015年6月第2次印刷
ISBN 978-7-5502-4904-2
定价：25.00元

未经许可，不得以任何方式复制或抄袭本书部分或全部内容
版权所有，侵权必究
本书若有质量问题，请与本公司图书销售中心联系调换。电话：010-82605388

目 录
CONTENTS

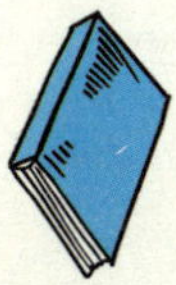

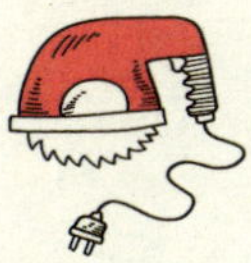

Are We Having Fun Yet

佚名 / Anonymous

为乐趣而生活

WILL I ENJOY DOING THIS?

我们都被洗脑了！我们被灌输了这样的“职业道德”：“工作（和忍受）到生命的最后一刻，如果你不能幸运地活到退休的话。我们没有时间浪费在无聊的事情上。我们有体现自身价值的责任。我们一定要认真而努力地工作，在事业上进步，赚更多的钱，并把赚钱和事业进步看做生活的首要目标。”

我希望变更自己的人生计划。我知道，做自己感兴趣的事，我会做得很好；做自己憎恶的事，我会做得一塌糊涂；在压力下工作，通常会事倍功半；在轻松的环境中做，同样的工作却会事倍功半。

我们可以改变生活中衡量某事是否该做的标准。我们需要扪心自问的不应是“它是否会赚大钱或能否让事业更上一层楼”，而是“我对这些感兴趣吗？这件事有意思吗？我要大干一番吗？”

如果你不能肯定地回答这些问题，那么，这些很有可能就不是你该做的事情！

如果是诸如纳税、洗碗等你必须做的事情，解决的办法就是找别人代你做，你不喜欢做的事情自然有人喜欢做。的确如此！举个例子来说，我并非世界上最棒的家庭主妇，我讨厌打扫卫生、擦地板和窗户等家务活，可偏偏有些人喜欢这种冥想性质的工作，并能在工作圆满完成后获得真正的满足。如果我雇人来做这些事，我就可以利用这些时间去做自己喜欢的事情来赚钱，这对我大有裨益。

人各有不同，不同的人适合做不同的事。某人喜欢做特定的某件事，这并不意味着你也必须要去喜欢。我所谓的“乐趣指数”可以用来帮助我们了解某一行业适合哪些人去做。判断一件事情是否该去做，不能只凭它能否带来物质利益和事业进步等经验主义，而应看此事是否能给我们带来乐趣并使我们获得满足感。你的工作带给你自豪感和满足感了吗？你是在执行“应该”指令，还是依照“想做”的意愿呢？

然而，这种程式是异常强大的。我发现，勉强自己做事的结果就是能拖则拖，没完没了。你留意过吗？做自己不喜欢的事情，似乎总也做不完。反之，则如俗语所云：“乐在其中，浑然不知所谓何日。”

我们要反对旧的程式，并相信“乐趣指数”是一个流动工程。每一个小的进步，同时也是一个大的飞跃。每一步都会淡化你对生活的不满情绪，强化你的自爱、自我认同和自尊感，让你更易感知生活中的乐趣。

不论何时，你都不能忽视这种内在激励。否则，你会日益陷入自厌与自责的泥潭，再次感到消沉没落。每一次失望都会强化心中的那个信念：别人的愿望比自己的更加重要。于是，你内在的欲求便会再次被压抑到最低位置。

但是，这就是你的生活！为何要让他人指示你“应该”怎样生活呢？问问你自己，你想怎样规划自己的人生！聆听内心的声音，它会告诉你什么会真正充实和满足你。要知道，你才是自己生活的主宰者！毕竟，这是你的生活，不是吗？

We've all been brainwashed! We were all taught the work ethic! "Work (and suffer) till you die, or if you're lucky retire. We don't have time to waste on frivolities. We have responsibilities to fulfill. We have to be serious, work hard, rise in our career, make lots of money, and make earning money and advancing in our career a priority."

I wish to change that programming in my life. I know that when I do the things I enjoy doing, things work out better for me. I know that when I do something against my will, against my heart, it doesn't work out well. I know that stressing myself out to try to get a job done usually takes twice as long as taking time out and doing that same task at some other time in a relaxed manner.

We can change the criteria by which we decide what to do in our lives. Instead of "Will it bring in lots of money or advance my career", we need to ask ourselves, "Will I enjoy doing this? Will this be fun? Am I looking forward to getting started on this?"

If you can't answer "yes" to these questions, then quite possibly this is not the task for you!

If it is something that must be done, i.e. taxes, dishes, etc, the solution is to find someone else to do them for you. There are some people who will enjoy and love to do what you prefer not to do. Really! For example, I am not the world's best housekeeper. I do not really enjoy cleaning, washing floors, windows, etc. Yet there are some people who enjoy the meditative aspect of this work and who really get satisfaction from a job well done. It is to my benefit to pay someone to do this work so I can take that time earning money doing things that I enjoy.

We are all very different and different things appeal to each one of us. Just because someone else enjoys a particular thing does not mean that you must. We can trust what I call the "fun index" to assist us in knowing if a particular action is the one for us. We can break away from the rule of thumb that judges things by whether they bring money or career advancement. We can change that to making our decisions based on whether an action will bring us pleasure and personal satisfaction. Does the work you do leave you feeling proud and pleased with yourself? Are you following the voice of "should"s or the one of "want to"?

Yet, the programming is strong. I find myself struggling over a task and it ends up dragging itself out. Have you noticed that the things that you dislike doing are the ones that seem to take forever to get done? As for the opposite viewpoint, well as the saying goes, "Time flies when you're having fun!"

Learning to go against that old programming and trusting the "fun index" is an ongoing project. Every small step is, at the same time, a big leap. Each step will move you away from dissatisfaction with your life and closer to self-love, self-acceptance, self-esteem and joy in your everyday existence.

Anytime you ignore that inner prompting, you accumulate self-loathing and disappointment in your being. Your inner child once again feels letdown and unimportant. Each letdown reinforce the inner child's belief that everybody else's wishes are more important than its own. Once again its desires are relegated to the lowest priority on the list.

Yet, it's your life! Why let someone else dictate how you "should" live it? Ask yourself what steps you want to take! Listen to the voice within which will tell you what would really make you feel fulfilled and satisfied. You are the boss of your life! After all, it's yours, isn't it?

THE PLEASURE OF READING

佚名 / Anonymous

读书的乐趣

人类世世代代的聪明才智，以及几百年来愉悦人们的故事，都可以轻松实惠地从书中获得。不过，我们必须懂得利用知识，进而获得最大收益。世上最不幸的人就是那些从未体会过阅读佳作所带来的快乐的人。

我对人很感兴趣，对他们本身和了解他们同样兴趣十足。我认识的一些卓越的人物只存在于作家的想象中，出现在作家的作品之中，最后变成我的想象。我从书中结识了新朋友，扩大了社会知识，也学到了新的语言。

如果说我是对人感兴趣，那么其他人则是关注方式方法而非人物。书中的人物可谓丰富多彩，不仅有科幻小说中描写的两万年后的超人，还可以追溯到历史上最早的人。方式方法则是千奇百怪的，包括对福尔摩斯侦探故事的巧妙叙述到科学发现和管教孩子的方法。

读书是一种精神享受，有点儿像体育运动。善于读书的人需要强烈的求知欲、丰富的知识和敏捷的反应。读书之所以是一种乐趣，并不在于作者告诉你什么，而是因为读书使你积极思考。在作者的引导下，你的想象任意驰骋，甚至超越

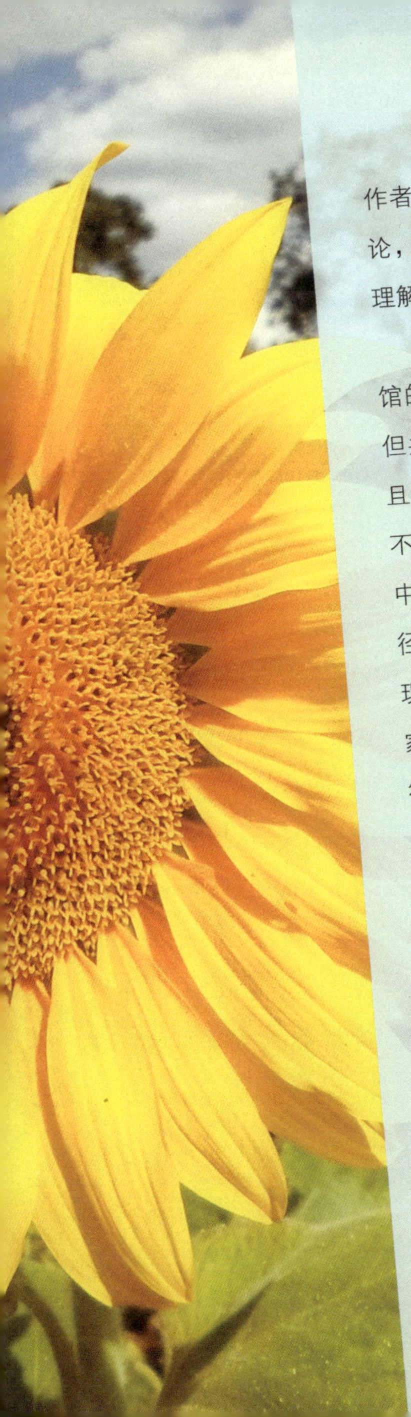

作者的想象。对比作者的经历，你会得出自己的结论，也许相同，也许相悖，而随着你对作者思想的理解，你也会变得越来越深刻。

每一部书都独自存在，犹如独户房子。而图书馆的书籍则像城市中的建筑。尽管它们各成一体，但共同构成一个整体。不仅它们之间相互关联，而且也与其他城市相互联系。相同或相近的看法会在不同的地方出现。文学作品中反映的就是人们生活中经常出现的事情，但在不同时期作者的处理大相径庭。书籍之间也相互影响，它们传承过去，体现现在，预测将来，相互联系，代代相传，形同各个家族。不管你从何时读起，都会有一种观点与你相符。长远来看，你不仅从书中了解世界，体验别人的生活，也会认识你自己。

只有你诚心读书，阅读才会成为一种乐趣。假如你读的是别人认为“该”读的书，你很可能觉得索然无味。假如你放下自己不喜欢的书，另试一本，直到发现自己觉得有意义的书，然后轻松地读下去，你肯定会感到心情畅快。假如你因阅读而变得更加高尚、聪明、善良和文雅，读书就不再是一种负担了。

All the wisdom of the ages, all the stories that have delighted mankind for centuries, are easily and cheaply available to all of us within the covers of books but we must know how to avail ourselves of this treasure and how to get the most from it. The most unfortunate people in the world are those who have never discovered how satisfying it is to read good books.

I am most interested in people, in them and finding out about them. Some of the most remarkable people I've met existed only in a writer's imagination, then on the pages of his book, and then, again, in my imagination. I've found in books new friends, new societies, new words.

If I am interested in people, others are interested not so much in who as in how. Who in the books includes everybody from science fiction superman two hundred centuries in the future all the way back to the first figures in history.How covers everything from the ingenious explanations of Sherlock Holmes to the discoveries of science and ways of teaching manner to children.

Reading is pleasure of the mind, which means that it is a little like a sport: your eagerness and knowledge and quickness make you a good reader. Reading is fun, not because the writer is telling you something, but because it makes your mind work. Your own imagination works along with the author's or even goes beyond his. Your experience, compared with his, brings you to the same or different conclusions, and your ideas develop as you understand his.

Every book stands by itself, like a one-family house, but books in a library are like houses in a city. Although they are separate, together they all add up to something, they are connected with each other and with other cities. The same ideas, or related ones, turn up in different places; the human problems that repeat themselves in life repeat themselves in literature, but with different solutions according to different writings at different times. Books influence each other; they link the past, the present and the future and have their own generations, like families. Wherever you start reading you connect yourself with one of the families of ideas, and in the long run, you not only find out about the world and the people in it; you find out about yourself, too.

Reading can only be fun if you expect it to be. If you concentrate on books somebody tells you you "ought" to read, you probably won't have fun. But if you put down a book you don't like and try another till you find one that means something to you, and then relax with it, you will almost certainly have a good time—and if you become, as a result of reading, better, wiser, kinder, or more gentle, you won't have suffered during the process.

假装的快乐

The Happy Door

[美] 米尔德里德·克拉姆 / Mildred Cram

快乐就像一枚鹅卵石突然掉入池塘中，激起一圈又一圈的涟漪，并不断向外围扩散。正如史蒂文森说的，快乐是一种责任。

快乐没有确切的定义。快乐的理由成千上万，而关键并不在于财富或健康。因为我们发现，乞丐、残疾人和所谓的失败者也能过得无比快乐。

快乐会有一种意想不到的收获，而保持快乐的心境是一种成就，是灵魂和性格的升华。事实上，追求快乐并非自私的表现，而是对自己和他人的一种责任。

郁闷就像一种传染病，人们往往对郁闷的人退避三舍。他们很快也会感到孤独、痛苦和难过。但是，有一种看似简单的治疗方法，虽然乍看似乎有些荒谬，如果你觉得不快乐，就假装快乐吧！

这个方法很管用，不久你就会发现，自己会吸引他人，而不是令人反感。你拥有一个以自我为中心的、日趋宽广的友好交际圈。这会是多么有益的事。

于是，假装的快乐就成为事实。你掌握了平和心境的秘诀，并且，在愉悦他人的过程中，自己也变得忘乎所以。

一旦意识到，保持快乐的心境是一种责任，并形成了习惯，它就能开启秘密花园的大门，那里云集着无数满怀感激的朋友。

Happiness is like a pebble dropped into a pool to set in motion an ever-widening circle of ripples. As Stevenson has said, being happy is a duty.

There is no exact definition of the word—happiness. Happy people are happy for all sorts of reasons. The key is not wealth or physical well-being, since we find beggars, invalids and so-called failures, who are extremely happy.

Being happy is a sort of unexpected dividend. But staying happy is an accomplishment, a triumph of soul and character. It is not selfish to strive for it. It is, indeed, a duty to us and others.

Being unhappy is like an infectious disease; it causes people to shrink away from the sufferer. He soon finds himself alone, miserable and embittered. There is, however, a cure so simple as to seem, at first glance, ridiculous: If you don't feel happy, pretend to be!

It works. Before long you will find that instead of repelling people, you attract them. You discover how deeply rewarding it is to be the center of wider and wider circles of good will.

Then the make-believe becomes a reality. You possess the secret of peace of mind, and can forget yourself in being of service to others.

Being happy, once it is realized as a duty and established as a habit, opens doors into unimaginable gardens thronged with grateful friends.

一切总会好的

佚名 / Anonymous

A Lesson of Life

每当我遇到困难时，母亲就对我说："如果你坚持下去，一切都会好的。不经历风雨，怎能见彩虹？"

直到1932年大学毕业，我才发现母亲是对的。当时，我已决意在电台谋求发展，努力成为一名体育节目播音员。我搭便车抵达芝加哥后，开始奔波于各个电台之间——但被一一拒绝。

一位在播音室里工作的好心女士告诉我，大型的电台是不会冒险接纳毫无经验的新人的——"到乡下去，找家能给你机会的小电台吧。"她说。

我乘车返回了家乡伊利诺伊州的迪克森。当时，家乡还没有电台播音员。父亲告诉我，蒙哥马利·沃德新开了家商店，正需要管理体育部的当地运动员。上中学时，我曾在迪克森打过橄榄球，于是我申请了这份工作。我似乎挺适合做这项工作的，结果却被拒绝了。

我失望极了。"一切总会好的。"母亲提醒我。为了方便找工作，父亲送了我一辆汽车。我去爱荷华州的达文波特，到当地电台求职。那里的电台节目总监，苏格兰人彼得·麦克阿瑟告诉我，播音员已有合适的人选。

当我走出他的办公室时，挫折感油然而生。我大声说道："如果在电台都找不到工作，又怎么能当体育节目的播音员呢？"

等电梯时，麦克阿瑟的声音传入我的耳畔："你说什么体育呢？你懂橄榄球吗？"然后，他让我站在话筒前，想象一场比赛，并为其解说。

去年秋天，我们的球队赢得了一场比赛——在最后20秒的时间里以65码的距离获胜，我用15分钟将那场精彩的比赛解说下来。彼得对我说，我可以解说周六的一场比赛。

回家途中，母亲的话又在我的耳边响起："坚持下去，一切都会好的。不经历风雨，怎能见彩虹？"我常想，当年，如果我能到蒙哥马利·沃德那里工作，我的人生又会驶向何方？

"Everything happens for the best," my mother said whenever I faced disappointment. "If you can carry on, one day something good will happen. And you'll realize that it wouldn't have happened if not for that previous disappointment."

Mother was right, as I discovered after graduating from college in 1932, I had decided to try for a job in radio, then work my way up to sports announcer. I hitchhiked to Chicago and knocked on the door of every station—and got turned down every time.

In one studio, a kind lady told me that big stations couldn't risk hiring inexperienced person—"Go out in the sticks and find a small station that'll give you a chance." she said.

I thumbed home to Dixon, Illinois. While there was no radio-announcing jobs in Dixon, my father said Montgomery Ward had opened a store and wanted a local athlete to manage its sports department. Since Dixon was where I had played high school football, I applied. The job sounded just right for me. But I wasn't hired.

My disappointment must have shown. "Everything happens for the best." Mom reminded me. Dad offered me the car to job hunt. I tried WOC Radio in Davenport, Iowa. The program director, a wonderful Scotsman named Peter MacArthur, told me they had already hired an announcer.

As I left his office, my frustration boiled over. I asked aloud, "How can a fellow get to be a sport announcer if he can't get a job in a radio station?"

I was waiting for the elevator when I heard MacArthur calling, "What was that you said about sports? Do you know anything about football?" Then he stood me before a microphone and asked me to broadcast an imaginary game.

The preceding autumn, my team had won a game in the last 20 seconds with a 65-yard run. I did a 15-minute buildup to that play, and Peter told me I would be broadcasting Saturday's game!

On my way home, as I have many times since, I thought of my mother's words, "If you carry on, one day something good will happen. Something wouldn't have happened if not for that previous disappointment." I often wonder what direction my life might have taken if I'd gotten the job at Montgomery Ward.

曲而不折地去生活

Bend,But Don't Break

佚名 / Anonymous

回想起童年，我最美好的回忆便是在小河边漫步，或懒懒地坐在河岸边。我可以静静地享受那份悠闲，看着流水潺潺，倾听着鸟鸣啾啾，树声萦耳。除此之外，我还喜欢看那片竹林。清风拂来，它们全都被压弯了腰；风势渐微，它们又都优雅地挺立起来，恢复之前的姿态。

每次我想到竹子从弯曲中重新挺拔身姿时，“韧性”一词便会在脑海中浮现。用这个词来描述人，即指此人轻松地从震惊、沮丧或其他心理极限的考验中恢复过来的能力。

你是否曾有过自己马上就要折断的感觉呢？是否曾有过自己已经到了崩溃边缘的感觉？感谢上帝，你历经磨难，现在才有机会去追忆那不堪回首的往事。

在那一段经历中，你也许感到交织的情绪正侵蚀着你的健康。你感到心灵麻木、脑力枯竭，甚至你正经受身体的各种不适。

人生跌宕起伏，悲欢交织。当不幸或痛苦再一次将你带到崩溃的边缘时，切记：曲而不折。努力吧，不要让这样的困境埋没杰出的你。

One of my fondest memories as a child is going by the river and sitting idly on the bank. There I would enjoy the peace and quiet, watch the water rush downstream, and listen to the chirps of birds and the rustling of leaves in the trees. I would also watch the bamboo trees bend under pressure from the wind and watch them return gracefully to their upright or original position after the wind had died down.

When I think about the bamboo tree's ability to bounce back or return to its original position, the word resilience comes to mind. When used in reference to a person this word means the ability to readily recover from shock, depression or any other situation that stretches the limits of a person's emotions.

Have you ever felt like you are about to snap? Have you ever felt like you are at your breaking point? Thankfully, you have survived the experience to live to talk about it.

During the experience you probably felt a mix of emotions that threatened your health. You felt emotionally drained, mentally exhausted and you most likely endured unpleasant physical symptoms.

Life is a mixture of good times and bad times, happy moments and unhappy moments. The next time you are experiencing one of those bad times or unhappy moments that take you close to your breaking point, bend but don't break. Try your best not to let the situation get the best of you.

快乐不必认真

The Importance of Doing Things Badly

佚名 / Anonymous

I. A. 威廉姆斯生于英格兰，在剑桥受过教育。第一次世界大战后，他成为伦敦《泰晤士报》的一名记者。威廉姆斯写了几本关于18世纪诗歌和戏剧方面的书，发表在各种期刊和杂志上，出版了他自己的诗集。以下这篇文章最早出现在1923年伦敦的《展望》一书中。

或许，对工作和创作而言，最大的威胁莫过于唯恐做得不好或者害怕做错。对于这个问题，这篇文章就是一种安慰了。威廉姆斯认为，很多事情都应该草草行事，这样，我们的生活才有意义，我们的个性才能得以发展完善。运动和音乐就是两个很好的例子，大多数人都酷爱运动和音乐，它们的确能给人带来乐趣，仅是这一点就够了，人们并不需要有多深的造诣。

查尔斯·拉姆写了一系列有关时下谬误的文章。可惜我一时记不清了。如果不是狡猾的仆人突然误导我，我倒不觉得他写过什么公众交口称赞而我却认为有害的文章。下面这句似是而非的忠告，我从孩提时就印在脑海中："如果一件事情值得去做，那么，就应该好好去做。"

从没有哪一个谬论让人们如此热衷。因为世界上有很多事情都值得去做，但并不是事事都应该好好去做。伟大的哲人赫伯特·斯宾塞曾对刚在台球桌上战胜他的年轻人说："先生，一般球技表现为好的眼力和稳定的手法，但从你的球技上看，你浪费了很多时间。"是否每一种游戏都值得持之以恒地练习和应用呢?

对职业运动员，我无话可说。他们是公众表演者，和其他人一样，他们通过自己在某项特定运动中的技术，至少可以实现人的首要社会责任——通过自己的合法劳动维持自己及家人的生活。但对于高明的业余爱好者，我们该怎么说呢？我认为，这些人是最应受到鄙视的。他们没有赚钱，仅仅为了自私的娱乐，就日复一日地投身于这种游戏。他们忽视了业余爱好者和专业人士之间合理的区别。最终他们为自己的技术所累，他们没做出任何对社会有价值的东西，没有垒起一块砖，没有犁过一亩地，没有写过一行文字，甚至没有通过劳动来养活全家和让自己受到教育。

不可否定，他们为某些人提供了娱乐，但他们一直没有勇气去参加测试。在这种测试中，我们需要每一个表演者证明他的职业选择是正确的——证明公众愿意为他的表演付费。当他们的辉煌期过去以后，不要说给整个世界留下什么，他们又给自己留下了什么呢？什么也没有留下，除了很快就会被遗忘的名字。也许他们的名字会被俱乐部里矮胖的绅士记住。

的确，玩游戏是一种并不值得好好去做的事情。但这并不是说全然不值得去做，就像前面的谚语暗示我们的一样。没有什么比玩自己喜欢的游戏更惬意和更有益的了，哪怕玩不好也不会影响真正喜欢它的人的心情。太在乎输赢的人并不是真正的运动爱好者——这个观点很对，但它的含义并没有被发掘。很少有人仅仅为了娱乐而玩游戏。为比赛而设的障碍为人们普遍接受，这不正好证明了这一点吗？为什么我们总是希望在自己的竞技能力之外额外得分呢？

“哦，但是，”我的读者也许会说，“弱一些的参赛者希望额外得分是为了促使强者有更好的表现。”但我并不这样认为。也许有时候，一个强壮但虚荣的参赛者希望给弱者额外加分，以使他的胜利更为显著。但我并不认为这是一个极好的解释。前些天去参加网球锦标赛时，我就把这种想法告诉了大赛秘书。“为什么要设置这些无聊的障碍呢？为什么不让我们尽情发挥呢？”我问他。“因为，”他回答道，“如果不设置这些障碍，就没有好一点儿的玩家参赛了。”这不就是承认了我们大多数人没有意识到草草行事的真正价值，还要固执己见、自欺欺人吗？

然而，并不是只有像游戏这样的小事才可以草草了之。虽然很奇怪，但事实是，我们易于接受草草地做某些事情，却不能接受草草地去做另一些事情。在我们认为可以草草去做的事情中，我举演戏为例，尽管演戏同其他表演艺术一样，会因其短暂性而减弱，但如果达到顶峰，也可以认为是一门伟大的艺术，一种值得好好去做的事情。演戏可以影响人类多变的情感，这就是演员所创造的东西——我们所说的表演艺术家是指能影响人类情感的有创造性的艺术家——是观众内心深处的一种印象、情感和思想，这是无法记录的。

所以，我认为，演戏可以称得上是一种艺术，虽然我只是简单地拿出了我的论据。然而，是否有人因为演得不好而不允许进入业余的戏剧表演呢？从来没有！因为演戏就像我写这篇短文一样，是一种可以草草去做的事情。

另一种就是音乐。那句谚语的谬误在音乐上得到了验证。然而，不知为何，它在演戏上并没有得到验证。很多人认为如果他们不能唱出很动听的歌，不能很娴熟地弹奏钢琴或者小提琴、竖琴，那么，他们最好不要去做这些事情。我承认，他们不应该不加选择地把低劣的表演给公众或者他们的熟人看。如果在家里也不能容忍这种低劣的音乐表演，这是我不赞成的。

没什么天赋的儿女，通过简单的歌声给他们的父母或不存在偏见的朋友带来快乐——这样的例子还少吗？然而有一天，这些小歌唱家开始因为不满足而苦恼。他们开始去学习音乐——如果他们资质平庸，性情温和——他们的局限就会暴露出来。十有八九，歌声就像一枚不值钱的硬币被抛在一边。有多少父亲为了鼓励女儿学歌而紧抓音乐不放？然而在教区音乐会上，她们可能会遭到打击。

在这里，我应该驻足观察一些奇怪的现象，有些人在画室或自家浴室从不唱歌，但在宗教集会或教堂里，他们会毫不犹豫地用那五音不全的嗓子放声高歌。我相信，要想回答这个问题，就得有一个完美的解释，但这属于神学的范畴，已经超出了我的研究范围。

“如果一件事值得去做，就应该好好去做”，这该死的说法就是导致个人生活极其匮乏的原因，从某种意义上讲，它也是公众生活水平降低的原因。这条谚语对资质平庸的人有两方面影响：它让资质平庸之辈不屑练习，而令资质超凡者为此付出很多，同时也将自己的思想强加给他人；它使人们疏于写作和写日记，同时也导致了本该锁在作者抽屉里的文集和日记的发表。

它导致了布兰克先生不去写诗——出于自娱自乐或与朋友的消遣，他可以写得很好的。同时，它也导致德茜小姐为了她那些并不成功的模仿之作（模仿德拉梅尔先生、叶芝先生和布里奇斯博士）而去纠缠各个杂志社疲惫的编辑们。结果是，现在，我们整个国家的艺术生活存在着两方面的迫切需求：更多的业余爱好者从事艺术实践，以及更高水平、更专业的艺术。只有达到这两个目标，我们才能获取心灵深处最美好的东西。

我认为，对我们来说，除去公民的职责，除去我们作为儿子、丈夫、父亲或者女儿、妻子、母亲的责任外，只有一件事情值得我们好好去做，值得我们全力以赴。这件事可以是写作、制造蒸汽机，也可以是砌砖块。除此之外，很多事我们都可以草草地去做，仅用我们的一部分精力，目的是为了放松自己或者触动自己的心灵。只有意识到这一点，人们才会幸福，才会满意，我们的家园才会更加美好。

我认为，有些事情草草去做可能比认真去做更好一些。比如钓鱼，其结果就是鱼儿被宰杀，一想到这些，钓鱼的乐趣就会荡然无存。当然，如果你既能钓到鱼又不去宰杀它，那就另当别论了。

I. A. Williams was born in England and educated at Cambridge. After World War I he served as a correspondent for the London Times. Williams wrote several books on eighteenth-century poetry and drama, published widely in journals and magazines, and published collections of his own poetry. The following article first appeared in London's The Outlook in 1923.

Perhaps the greatest threat to productivity in both work and play is the fear of doing things badly or wrong. This article offers some comfort. Williams points out that there are many things worth doing badly, and that our lives are enriched and our personalities enhanced by these activities. Two central examples, sports and music, are valuable to most people in proportion to how enthusiastically they do them, rather than how well.

Charles Lamb wrote a series of essays upon popular fallacies. I do not, at the moment, carry them very clearly in my memory; but, unless that treacherous servant misleads me more even than she usually does, he did not write of one piece of proverbial so-called wisdom that has always seemed to me to be peculiarly pernicious. And this saw, this scrap of specious advice, this untruth masquerading as logic, is one that I remember to have had hurled at my head at frequent intervals from my earliest youth right up to my present advanced age. How many times have I not been told that "If a thing is worth doing at all, it is worth doing well"?

Never was there a more untruthful word spoken in earnest. For the world is full of things that are worth doing, but certainly not worth doing well. Was it not so great a sage as Herbert Spencer who said to the young man who had just beaten him at billiards, "Moderate skill, sir, is the sign of a good eye and a steady hand, but skill such as yours argues a youth misspent?" Is any game worth playing supremely well, at the price of constant practice and application?

Against the professional player I say nothing; he is a public entertainer, like any other, and by his skill in his particular sport he at least fulfills the first social duty of man—that of supporting himself and his family by his own legitimate exertions. But what is to be said of the crack amateur? To me he seems one of the most contemptible of mankind. He earns no money, but devotes himself, for the mere selfish pleasure of the thing, to some game, which he plays day in day out; he breaks down the salutary distinction between the amateur and the professional; eventually his skill deserts him, and he leaves behind him nothing that is of service to his fellow men—not a brick laid, not an acre ploughed, not a line written, not even a family supported and educated by his labor.

It is true that he has provided entertainment for a certain number of persons, but he has never had the pluck to submit himself to the test by which we demand that every entertainer should justify his choice of a calling—the demonstration of the fact that the public is willing to pay him for his entertainment. And, when his day is over, what is left, not even to the world, but to himself? Nothing but a name that is at once forgotten, or is remembered by stout gentlemen in clubs.

The playing of games, certainly, is a thing which is not worth doing well. But that does not prove that it is not worth doing at all, as the proverb would, by implication, persuade us. There is nothing more agreeable and salutary than playing a game which one likes, and the circumstance of doing it badly interferes with the pleasure of no real devotee of any pastime. The man who minds whether or not he wins is no true sportsman—which observation is trite, but the rule it implies is seldom observed, and comparatively few people really play games for the sheer enjoyment of the playing. Is this not proved by the prevalence and popularity of handicaps? Why should we expect to be given points unless it be that we wish to win by means other than our own skill?

"Ah! but," my reader may say, "the weaker player wants to receive points in order that he may give the stronger one a better game." Really, I do not believe that that is so. Possible, sometimes, a strong and vainglorious player may wish to give points, in order that his victory may be the more notable. But I do not think that even this is the true explanation. That, I suspect, was given to me the other day by the secretary of a lawn-tennis tournament, in which I played. "Why all this nonsense of handicaps? Why not let us be squarely beaten, and done with it?" I asked him. "Because," He replied, "if we did not give handicaps, none of the less good players would enter." Is that not a confession that the majority of us have both realized the true value doing a trivial thing badly, for its own sake, and must needs have our minds buoyed and cheated into a false sense of excellence?

Moreover it is not only such intrinsically trivial things as games that are worth doing badly. This is a truth which, oddly enough, we accept freely of some things—but not of others—and as a thing which we are quite content to do will let me instance acting. Acting, at its best, can be a great art, a thing worth doing supremely well, though its worth, like that of all interpretative arts, is lessened by its evanescence. For it works in the impermanent medium of human flesh and blood, and the thing that the actor create—for what we call an interpretative artist is really a creative artist working in a perishable medium—is an impression upon, an emotion or a thought aroused in, the minds of an audience, and is incapable of record.

Acting, then, let me postulate—though I have only sketched ever so briefly the proof of my belief—can be a great art. But is anyone ever deterred from taking part in amateur theatricals by the consideration that he cannot act well? Not a bit of it! And quite rightly not, for acting is one of the things about which I am writing this essay—the things that are worth doing badly.

Another such thing is music; but here the proverbial fallacy again exerts its power, as it does not, for some obscure and unreasoning discrimination, in acting. Most people seem to think that if they cannot sing, or play the piano, fiddle, or sackbut, admirably well, they must not do any of these things at all. That they should not indiscriminately force their inferior performances upon the public, or even upon their acquaintances, I admit. But that there is no place "in the home" for inferior musical performances, is an untruth that I flatly deny.

How many sons and daughters have not, with a very small talent, given their parents—and even the less fondly prejudiced ears of their friends—great pleasure with the singing of simple songs? Then one day there comes to the singer the serpent of dissatisfaction; singing lessons are taken, and—if the pupil is of moderate talent and modest disposition—limitations are discovered. And then, in nine cases out of ten, the singing is dropped, like a hot penny. How many fathers have not banished music from their homes by encouraging their daughters to take singing lessons? Yet a home may be the fresher for singing that would deserve brickbats at a parish concert.

I may pause here to notice the curious exception that people who cannot on any account be persuaded to sing in the drawing-room, or even in the bath, will without hesitation uplift their tuneless voices at religious meetings or in church. There is a perfectly good and honorable explanation of this, I believe, but it belongs to the realm of metaphysics and is beyond my present scope.

This cursed belief, that if a thing is worth doing at all, it is worth doing well, is the cause of a great impoverishment in our private life, and also, to some extent, of the lowering of standards in our public life. For this tenet of proverbial faith has two effects on small talents: It leads modest persons not to exercise them at all, and immodest persons to attempt to do so too much and to force themselves upon the public. It leads to the decay of letter-writing and of the keeping of diaries, and, as surely, it leads to the publication of memoirs and diaries that should remain locked in the writers'desks.

It leads Mr. Blank not to write verses at all—which he might very well do, for the sake of his own happiness, and for the amusement of his friends—and it leads Miss Dash to pester the overworked editors of various journals with her unsuccessful imitations of Mr. de la Mare, Mr. Yeats, and Dr. Bridges.The result is that our national artistic life now suffers from two great needs: A wider amateur practice of the arts, and a higher, more exclusive, professional standard. Until these are achieved we shall not get the best out of our souls.

The truth is, I conceive, that there is for most of us only one thing—beyond, of course, our duties of citizenship and our personal duties as sons, or husbands, or fathers, daughters, or wives, or mothers—that is worth doing well—that is to say, with all our energy. That one thing may be writing, or it may be making steam-engines, or laying bricks. But after that there are hundreds of things that are worth doing badly, with only part of our energy, for the sake of the relaxation they bring us, and for the contacts which they give us with our minds. And the sooner England realizes this, as once she did, the happier, the more contented, the more gracious, will our land be.

There are even, I maintain, things that are in themselves better done badly than well. Consider fishing, where one's whole pleasure is often spoiled by having to kill a fish. Now, if one could contrive always to try to catch a fish, and never to do so, one might—But that is another story.

享受花朵和蜂蜜的快乐

On Pleasure

[美]卡里·纪伯伦 / Kahlil Gibran

快乐是一首自由的歌，但它不是自由。它是你们的欲望绽放的花朵，但不是它们的果实；它是深谷对高峰的呼唤，但它既不深沉也不高耸；它是囚禁在笼中展翅的鸟儿，而不是环抱的空间。哦，的确，快乐是首自由的歌！我愿你们全心全意地歌唱它，但不愿你们在歌唱时迷失自己的心。

年轻人中有一些人追求快乐，好像它就是一切，他们已经受到判决和谴责。我不会判决他们，也不会谴责他们，我会让他们去寻找。因为他们寻找的是快乐，然而也不单单是快乐；快乐有七个姐妹，她们中最小的也比她柔美。难道你们不曾听说，有人在刨树根时发现了宝藏吗？

老年人中有一些人遗憾地回忆快乐，好像在追悔酒醉后做的错事。遗憾只会让心灵蒙上阴影，而不是一种惩罚。他们应以感恩之心回忆他们的快乐，好像回忆夏日的收获。如果遗憾能给他们以慰藉，那就让他们得到安慰吧。

还有一些人，既不是喜欢追寻的年轻人，又不是沉湎于回忆的老年人。他们在追寻和回忆的恐惧中逃避一切快乐，唯恐自己忽视或惹怒了心灵。

然而，在他们的前行中也有快乐。

因而，即使他们用颤抖的双手挖掘树根，也会找到宝藏。

请告诉我，谁敢惹怒灵魂呢?

夜莺会扰乱夜的寂静，萤火虫会惹恼繁星吗?你们的火焰和烟雾会拖累风吗?

你们以为灵魂是一汪止水，你们用一根木棍就可以搅乱吗?你们通常拒绝快乐，你们只是把快乐的欲望潜伏在内心中。

有谁知道，今天被忽略的事，明天会不会存在?甚至你们的身体也了解它的本性和合理需求，而不会被欺骗。

你们的身体是心灵的琴弦，它或奏出柔美的乐曲，或拨弄出混乱的噪音，全都在你。

现在你们扪心自问："我们将怎样区别快乐中的善与恶呢?"去你们的田野和花园，你们就会明白蜜蜂的快乐在于采集花蜜;对于花朵而言，给蜜蜂提供花蜜就是快乐。因为蜜蜂视花朵为生命之泉，而花朵视蜜蜂为爱之使者。对于两者而言，蜜蜂与花朵，给予与接受的快乐是一种需要和狂喜的快乐。

奥菲里斯城的人们，尽情享受快乐吧，就像花朵和蜜蜂一样!

Pleasure is a freedom song, but it is not freedom. It is the blossoming of your desires; but it is not their fruit; it is a depth calling unto a height, but it is not the deep nor the high; it is the caged taking wing, but it is not space encompassed. Ay, in very truth, pleasure is a freedom song. And I fain would have you sing it with fullness of heart; yet I would not have you lose your hearts in the singing.

Some of your youth seek pleasure as if it was all, and they are judged and rebuked. I would not judge nor rebuke them. I would have them seek, for they shall find pleasure, but not her alone; seven are her sisters, and the least of them is more beautiful than pleasure. Have you not heard of the man who was digging in the earth for roots and found a treasure?

And some of your elders remember pleasures with regret like wrongs committed in drunkenness. But regret is the beclouding of the mind and not its chastisement. They should remember their pleasures with gratitude, as they would remember the harvest of a summer. Yet if it comforts them to regret, let them be comforted.

And there are among you those who are neither young to seek nor old to remember; and in their fear of seeking and remembering they shun all pleasures, lest they neglect the spirit or offend against it.

But even in their foregoing is their pleasure.

And thus they also find a treasure though they dig for roots with quivering hands.

But tell me, who is he that can offend the spirit?

Shall the nightingale offend the stillness of the night, or the firefly the stars? And shall your flame or your smoke burden the wind?

Thank you the spirit is a still pool which you can trouble with a staff? Oftentimes in denying yourself pleasure you do but store the desire in the recesses of your being.

Who knows but that which seem omitted today, waits for tomorrow? Even your body knows its heritage and its rightful need and will not be deceived.

And your body is the harp of your soul, and it is yours to bring forth sweet music from it or confused sounds.

And now you ask in your heart, "How shall we distinguish that which is good in pleasure from that which is not good?" Go to your fields and your gardens and you shall learn that it is the pleasure of the bee to gather honey of the flower, but it is also the pleasure of the flower to yield its honey to the bee, for to the bee a flower is a fountain of life, and to the flower a bee is a messenger of love, and to both, bee and flower, the giving and the receiving of pleasure is a need and an ecstasy.

People of Orphalese, be in your pleasures like the flowers and the bees.

[美] 理查德·沃克尔默 / Richard Wolkomir

简单生活

The Art of Living Simply

那一年，九月的下午，我们五对夫妇各自慢悠悠地划着独木舟，沿着缅因州的萨科河顺流而下，沐浴在夏末的金色阳光之中，无比惬意。岸边的小鹿，啃着小草，摇着白色的尾巴，注视着我们这支小小的船队漂流而过。晚上，我们搭起了帐蓬，烤着牛排，围着篝火懒散地躺着，睡眼朦胧地凝望着满天繁星。有人弹拨着吉它，唱起古老的歌曲："淡泊乃是天资，自由乃是天赐。"

当然了，田园牧歌式的漫游告一段落，我们又驱车回到这个世界，还贷款，忙工作，还有洗衣机塞满了脏衣服。偶尔我也会情不自禁地哼唱："淡泊乃是天资，自由乃是天赐。"我多想活得淡定从容，可哪儿去找呢?

"我们的生命都因为繁杂琐事尽付东流。简单点，简单点。"亨利·戴维·梭罗的警世名言打从老牛犁地、汽船轰鸣的时代就萦绕耳畔，挥之不去。而梭罗自己也不过在瓦尔登湖边自己造的小木屋里度过两年光阴，他无妻，无子，无所事事——不必为利率高低不同的房屋按揭这类繁杂琐事费劲操劳。

我的生活总被繁杂琐事吸引，好像我的座右铭该是"复杂点，复杂点"。我还发现我并非唯一。然而有一天，我对简单朴素的想法完全颠覆了。

有一天，我去拜访一位物理学家，他的办公室是一座塔楼，矗立于他的家乡伊利诺伊州农场之上。透过窗户，我们看到塔楼下远处的草场上有一座巨大的圆形物——那是实验室方圆几英里的粒子加速器，他解释说："这是一种时间机器。"加速器使得物理学家们能够对混沌初开时的状况加以研究。他补充说，那时的宇宙要简单一些，或许只是一个小圆点，只包含一种能量或一种粒子。而现在的宇宙有着多种能量和几十种粒子，从星球、银河系到蒲公英、大象和济慈的诗文，包罗万象。

就在那个塔楼上，我方才明白：复杂，乃是上帝全盘设计的一部分。

在内心深处，我们感觉到这一点。每每谈到"头脑简单的傻子"时，我们常常带着轻蔑的口吻。谁也不想背上一个"简单化"的罪名。

但对复杂的状态视而不见是危险的。我曾经买过一所房子，由于非常喜欢周围环境，不知不觉之间忽略了可能存在的缺点。房子归我之后，我才发现，要做的事情不胜枚举：需要隔热保温，需要加盖屋顶，需要新的供暖系统，需要新窗户，需要新的化粪池。房子让我不堪重负，修缮的高额费用令我力有不

速，而精神压力则更大，这便是我不愿正视复杂性的后果。

就连一般的财务问题也不是那么简单，譬如，你的保险单上究竟包括了哪些条款？然而，与道德问题相比，经济学本身还算是简洁明了。

记得十岁那年有一天下午，我无意中成了一帮孩子的校外头目。我知道要马上干一件让他们兴奋的事儿，不然，我这个位子难保。正在此时，我看到了乔。

在孩子里，乔是一个小巨人，高得像埃菲尔铁塔。他们全家从欧洲移民过来，因此他略微有些乡音。

"捉住他！"我叫道。

我这支野蛮的小部队一窝蜂地向乔扑了上去，有人抢走了他的帽子，我们就玩起传球接球游戏。乔跑回家，我拿着他的帽子，活像缴获了一个战利品。

那天晚上，我家的门铃响了。乔的父亲，一个愁容满面、口音浓重的农夫上门讨还乔的帽子，我局促不安地还给了他。"请不要再招惹乔了，"他郑重其事地对我说："他有哮喘病，发作起来很难好的。"

我感到胸口像塞进了一个铅做的垒球。第二天晚上，我走到乔的家，他正在花园里翻土。我走近他，他则警惕地望着我。我问是否能帮上点儿忙。"好吧，"他回答说。从那以后，我经常去帮他，我们成了最要好的朋友。

我向成熟迈进了一步。我在自己身上看到了各种各样的可能性，就像一团缠结不清的电线。红线通向邪恶，要的不过是对他人的痛苦不理不睬。而白线通向悲天悯人。我的手可能触及所有的电线——一切取决于我所作的决定。我已发现了事物的复杂，其本身是一种机会，我们借此做出选择，得以成长，代价便是承担责任。

也许，这正是我们渴望淡泊简朴生活的一个理由。在某种意义上，我们情愿做个孩子，好让其他人背负责任，穷于应付。

像小麦一样，我们在这块土地上等待成熟。心智上的成熟要靠尽量吸取宇宙万物的复杂性；道德上的成熟有赖于作出决断，有所取舍；精神上的成熟则要凭借我们张大双眼目睹造物主带给我们的繁杂琐事，无穷无尽。

一天下午，我在院子里拾起一片枫树的落叶，近看是黄的，带点红色，斑斑驳驳。伸直胳膊再看，便成了桔黄色，它的颜色决定于我怎么看它。

我对这片叶子的经历略有所知，它吸收阳光，把二氧化碳转化为养料。我知道我们动物所吸入的氧气是这些植物吐出来的，而它们则靠我们呼出的二氧化碳茁壮成长。我还知道，叶子的每一个细胞都有一个脱氧核糖核酸的细胞核，上面刻写着一切关于枫树怎样形成和变化的指令。这一点科学家们比我知道的多得多，但就是他们的知识也不过是对枫树这复杂的知识海洋的浅辄探索而已。

我觉着开始懂得简单朴素的真正意义了。这并不意味着无视那令人眼花缭乱的缤纷世界，或是逃避使我们成熟的选择。“简单点，简单点。”梭罗所指的是简化我们自己。

要做到这一点，可以参照以下几点：

关注意义深远的事务。生活得淡泊不一定非要住小屋、种豆子不可。它只是使我们的生命不至于“因为繁杂琐事尽付东流”。有位教授告诉我集中精力的秘诀：“关掉电视，阅读伟大的书籍，它们会为你们打开一扇智慧的大门。”

人生之旅步步为营。有一次曾遇到一对夫妇，他俩天生是盲人，有一个三岁女儿和一个婴儿，两个孩子都视力完好。对这样的父母来

说，每件事情都是复杂的：给婴儿洗澡，管教女儿，修剪草坪。然而，他们的生活却充满了欢声笑语。我问这位母亲怎样跟踪她那活泼可爱的女儿，她笑着回答："我在她的鞋子上系上了小铃铛。"

"那么等小婴儿也会走路了，怎么办呢？"我又问。

她微笑着说："每件事都那么复杂，所以不到万不得已，我不会试着去解决某个问题。我每次只承担一件事情！"

降低我们的欲望。英国小说家、戏剧家杰罗姆·克拉普卡的一番话道出了其个人胆识的精神本质。他写道："让你的生命之舟轻巧些，只装上你需要的东西——一个朴实的家，简单恬淡的快乐，一二知己，你爱的人和爱你的人，一只猫，一条狗，烟斗一二，够吃的食品，够穿的衣服，饮料多带一些，因为口干舌燥可是要人命呢。"

不久前，我乘飞机回乡看望住院的父亲，他得了一种记忆逐渐丧失的疾病。我心如乱麻，忧虑忡忡：如何治疗？如何护理？经济负担又如何？

父亲蜷缩在轮椅上，萎靡不振。我从前所熟知的父亲面容苍白，已是枯叶飘零，风烛残年。我站在那儿，痛苦迷茫。忽然间，父亲抬起双眼，看到了我。就在那一刹，我在父亲的眼睛里看到了令人惊奇的神采：他认出了我，眼神中充满了爱。父亲老泪纵横，我也是热泪盈眶。

那天下午，父亲似乎从病魔那儿回来了。他玩笑不断，笑声朗朗，我又一回看到我所熟悉的父亲。然后他疲惫不堪，我们把他抱回床上。第二天，他完全不记得我来看过他。第三天夜里便与世长辞。

每一个死亡都是通往神秘造物主的一扇大门，大门开了，但我们所见的只是一片黑暗。在那令人敬畏的时刻，我们意识到，宇宙是多么的浩瀚无穷，繁复杂驳，令人匪夷所思。然而，领悟淡泊生活真正的聪颖天资就在于能够接受世界无穷无尽的错综复杂，接受纷乱困惑。

淡泊简朴的生活尤其需要细细品尝。一张我们所钟爱的面庞，或许，一双闪耀着爱意的眼睛。

虽平淡无奇，却令人回味不尽。

We paddled down Maine's Saco River that September afternoon, five couples in canoes, basking in the summer's last golden sunlight. Grazing deer, fluttering their white tails, watched our flotilla pass. That evening we pitched tents, broiled steaks and sprawled around the campfire, staring sleepily at the stars. One man, strumming his guitar, sang an old Shaker song: "Tis the gift to be simple. Tis the gift to be free."

Our idyll ended, of course, and we drove back to the world of loan payments, jobs and clogged washing machines." Tis the gift to be simple," I found myself humming at odd moments, " Tis the gift to be free." How I longed for that simplicity. But where could I find it?

"Our life is frittered away by detail. Simplify, simplify." That dictum of Henry David Thoreau's, echoing from the days of steamboats and ox-drawn plows, had long hunted me. Yet Thoreau himself was able to spend only two years in the cabin he built beside Walden Pond. And Henry—wifeless, childless, jobless—never had to tussle with such details as variable-rate mortgages.

My life attracted detail, as if my motto were: "Complicate, complicate." And I've found I'm not alone. But one day my thinking about simplicity turned upside down.

I was visiting a physicist in his office tower jutting from his Illinois farmlands. We looked through his window at the laboratory's miles—around particle accelerator, an immense circle in the prairie far below. "It's a kind of time machine," he said, explaining that the accelerator enables physicists to study conditions like those shortly after Creation's first moment. The universe was simpler then, he noted, a mere dot comprising perhaps only one kind of force and one kind of particle. Now it has many kinds of forces, scores of different particles, and contains everything from stars and galaxies to dandelions, elephants and the poems of Keats.

Complexity, I began to see from that tower, is part of God's plan.

Deep down, we sense that we speak, disparagingly, of a "simpleton". Nobody wants to be guilty of "simplistic" thinking.

But blinding ourselves to complexity can be dangerous. Once I bought a home. I liked its setting so much I unconsciously avoided probing into its possible defects. After it was mine, I found it needed insulation, roofing, a new heating system, new windows, a new septic system—everything. That old house became an albatross, costing far more than I could afford; the cost in stress was even higher. I had refused to look at the complexities.

Even ordinary finances are rarely simple—what does your insurance policy actually cover? Yet, economics are simplicity itself compared with moral questions.

One afternoon when I was ten, I found myself the leader of an after-school gaggle of boys. I had to divert them quickly, I knew, or my career as leader would be brief. And then I saw Joe.

Joe was an Eiffel Tower of a kid, an incipient giant. His family had emigrated from Europe, and he had a faint accent.

"Let's get him!" I said.

My little troop of Goths swarmed upon Joe. Somebody snatched his hat and we played catch with it. Joe ran home, and I took his hat as a trophy.

That night, our doorbell rang. Joe's father, a worried-looking farmer with a thick accent, asked for Joe's hat. I returned it sheepishly. "Please don't upset Joe," he said earnestly. "He has asthma. When he has an attack, it is hard for him to get better."

I felt a lead softball in my chest. The next evening I walked to Joe's house. He was in the garden, tilling the soil; he watched me warily as I walked up. I asked if I could help. "Okay," he said. After that I went often to help him and we became best friends.

I had taken a step toward adulthood. Inside myself I had seen possibilities, like a tangle of wires. This red wire was the possibility for evil, which requires no more than ignoring another's pain. And here was the white wire of sympathy. I could have a hand in connecting all those wires—it was a matter of the decisions I made. I had discovered complexity, and found in it an opportunity to choose, to grow. Its price is responsibility.

Perhaps, that is one reason why we yearn for the simple life. In a way, we want to be children, to let someone else carry the awkward backpack of responsibility.

We are like wheat, here on earth to ripen. We ripen intellectually by letting in as much of the universe's complexity as we can. Morally we ripen by making our choices. And we ripen spiritually by opening our eyes to Creation's endless detail.

One afternoon I picked up a fallen leaf from the sugar maple in our yard. Up close it was yellow, with splashes of red. At arm's length it was orange. Its color depended on how I looked at it.

I knew a little about how this leaf had spent its life, transforming sunlight and carbon dioxide into nutrients, and I knew that we animals breathe that oxygen that such plants emit, while they thrive upon the carbon dioxide we exhale. And I knew that each cell of the leaf has a nucleus containing a chemical—DNA—upon which is inscribed all the instructions for making and operating a sugar maple. Scientists know far more about this than I. But even their knowledge extends only a short way into the sea of complexity that is a sugar maple.

I'm beginning to understand, I think, what simplicity means. It does not mean blinding ourselves to the world's stunning complexity or avoiding the choices that ripen us. By "simplify, simplify." Thoreau meant simplifying ourselves.

To accomplish this, we can:

Focus on deeper things. The simple life is not necessarily living in a cabin, cultivating beans. It is refusing to let our lives be "frittered away by detail". A professor taught me a secret for focusing: Turn off the TV and read great books. They open doors in your brain.

Undertake life's journey one step at a time. I once met a young couple both blind since birth. They had a three-year-old daughter and an infant, both fully sighted. For those parents, everything was complex: bathing the baby, monitoring their daughter, mowing the lawn. Yet, they were full of smiles and laughters. I asked the mother how she kept track of their lively daughter. "I tie little bells on her shoes," she said with a laugh.

"What will you do when the infant walks too?" I asked.

She smiled. "Everything is so complicated that I don't try to solve a problem until I have to. I take one thing at a time!"

Pare down your desires. English novelist and playwright Jerome Klapka caught the spirit of that enterprise when he wrote, "Let your boat of life be light, packed only with what you need—a homely home and simple pleasures, one or two friends, worth the name, someone to love and someone to love you, a cat, a dog and a pipe too, enough to eat and enough to wear and a little more than enough to drink, for thirst is a dangerous thing."

Not long ago I flew home to see my father in hospital. He has a disease that nibbles away the mind. I was a snarl of worries. Treatments?Nursing homes?Finances?

He was crouched in a wheelchair, a shriveled, whitened remnant of the father I had known. As I stood there, hurt and confused, he looked up and saw me. And then I saw something unexpected and wonderful in his eyes: recognition and love. It welled up and filled his eyes with tears. And mine.

That afternoon, my father came back from wherever his illness had taken him. He joked and laughed, once again the man I had known. And then he was tired, and we put him to bed. The next day, he did not remember I had come. And the next night he died.

Every death is a door opening on Creation's mystery. The door opens, but we see only darkness. In that awful moment, we realize how vast the universe is, complexity upon complexity, beyond us. But that is the true gift of simplicity: to accept the world's infinite complication, to accept bewilderment.

And then, especially, we can savor simple things. A face we love, perhaps, eyes brimming with love.

It is the simplest of things. But it is more than enough.

放轻松 佚名 / Anonymous

Lighten up

最近这段时间，我们所有人看起来似乎都有些过于严肃。我的大女儿时不时地对我说："爸，瞧你又板着脸了。"即使是我们当中那些刻意乐观的人，恐怕也是太过严肃了。任何一件小事都可以让我们沮丧、恼火——自己迟到了五分钟，别人晚到了五分钟，交通堵塞，别人误解了我们或者说错了什么，支付账单，排队，烧糊了一顿饭，犯了一个实实在在的错误——不计其数。生活真的就是这样的小事都能让我们方寸大乱。

或许本杰明·富兰克林说得最具体："我们局限的视角，还有我们的希望和恐惧成为我们评价生活的标尺，只要出现的情形违背了我们的想法，它们就会变成我们的困扰。"我们一生都在期望事事如愿——而当事事不尽如人意时，我们便会反抗，便会为此折磨自己。

改掉过于严肃的心态的第一步是承认你有问题。你不得不有所改变，变得轻松一点儿。你一定要意识到烦躁的心情在很大程度上是你自己造成的——不管是你自己设定的生活方式，还是你对事物的反应方式。

第二步是了解你的期望值和失望感之间的联系。一旦你所期望的事情没有实现，你就会沮丧、痛苦。同样的，当你抛开过多的期望，当你接受生活本来的样子，你便获得了自由。太过执著的期望必然导致严肃紧绷，敢于放手才能怡然自得。

早晨醒来便下决心在一天里对任何人或事都不抱任何期望，这是一种很好的练习。不要期望人们都是友好的，不要期望这一天能够一帆风顺。这样，当遇到问题时，对自己说：“啊，又有一个需要跨越的障碍。”如果你用这种心态来迎接每一天，你就会发现生活原本是多么美好。与其反抗现实，还不如与它“共舞”。随着不断地练习，过不了多久，你就会让自己的整个生活更加轻松愉快。当你感到愉悦时，生活会变得更加丰富多彩。

These days, it seems that almost all of us are too serious. My older daughter often says to me, "Daddy, you've got that serious look again."Even those of us who are committed to non-seriousness are probably too serious. People are frustratedand uptight about virtually everything—being five minutes late, having someone else show up five minutes late, being stuck in traffic, witnessing someone look at us wrong or say the wrong thing, paying bills, waiting in line, overcooking a meal, making an honest mistake—you name it, we all lose perspective over it.

Life is simply as it is. Perhaps Benjamin Franklin said it best: "Our limited perspective, our hopes and fears become our measure of life, and when circumstances don't fit our ideas, they become our difficulties."We spend our lives wanting things,people, and events to be just as we want them to be—and when they're not, we fight and we suffer.

The first step in recovering from over seriousness is to admit that you have a problem. You have to want to change, to become more easygoing. You have to see that your own uptightness is largely of your own creation—it's composed of the way you have set up your life and the way you react to it.

The next step is to understand the link between your expectations and your frustration level. Whenever you expect something to be a certain way and it isn't, you're upset and you suffer. On the other hand, when you let go of your expectations, when you accept life as it is, you're free. To hold on is to be serious and uptight. To let go is to lighten up.

A good exercise is to try to approach a single day without expectations. Don't expect people to be friendly. Don't expect your day to be problem free. Instead, as problems come up, say to yourself, "Ah, another hurdle to overcome."As you approach your day in this manner you'll notice how graceful life can be. Rather than fighting against life, you'll be dancing with it. Pretty soon, with practice, you'll lighten up your entire life. And when you lighten up, life is a lot more fun.

切勿等待

佚名 / Anonymous

Now Is the Best Time to Be Happy

我们安慰自己，生活会随着结婚，有了一两个孩子而更加美满。然而，孩子尚小时，他们会把我们弄得焦头烂额，只有当他们长大后，我们才能感到心满意足。

之后，我们又会对十几岁孩子的问题感到束手无策。只有当他们走过这一时期，我们才会真正幸福愉快。我们告诉自己，当爱人始终如一地给予我们支持；当我们获得了漂亮的汽车，能够进行一次愉快的旅行；或者当我们退休后，那时的生活才称得上完美。

事实上，没有比“现在”更令人幸福的时光。如果不是“现在”，又会是何时呢？最好接受“人生充满挑战”这一事实，并决定无论怎样，都要让自己快乐。

幸福是一段旅程。因此，要珍爱你拥有的每刻，更要珍视那些与你分享时光的特别之人。谨记，岁月不待人。

所以，切勿等待！

人生中没有比现在更快乐的时光。

幸福是一段旅程，而非目的地。

尽情工作吧，就像你根本不需要钱；放手去爱吧，就像你从未受过伤；纵情舞蹈吧，就像无人观看。

We convince ourselves that life will be better after we get married, have a baby, then another. Then we are frustratedthat the kids aren't old enough and we'll be more content when they are grown up.

After that, we're frustrated that we have teenagers to deal with. We will certainly be happy when they are out of that stage. We tell ourselves that our life will be complete when our spouse gets his or her act together, when we get a nicer car, and are able to go on a nice vacation. Or when we retire.

The truth is, there's no better time to be happy than right now. If not now, when? Your life will always be filled with challenges. It's best to admit this to yourself and decide to be happy anyway.

Happiness is the way. So, treasure every moment that you have and treasure it more because you shared it with someone special, special enough to spend your time with him, and remember that time waits for no one.

So, stop waiting.

There is no better time than right now to be happy.

Happiness is a journey, not a destination.

So, work like you don't need money; love like you've never been hurt; and dance like no one's watching.

你的生活自己决定

You Have a Choice

▶ 佚名 / Anonymous

清晨，我早早醒来，为自己在午夜的钟声敲响前将要做的一切激动不已。我有责任让今天过得充实，我的作用是很重要的。

选择如何度过每一天，这是我的工作。

今天下雨了，所以我可以抱怨；但是，草地无需花费力气去浇灌，所以我还可以感激。

今天没有足够的钱，所以我可以难过；但这也使我懂得理性消费，引导我远离浪费，所以我也可以欣喜。

今天为自己的健康问题，我可以满腹牢骚；但自己仍然活着，所以我可以欢呼雀跃。

今天因为小时候父母给予的太少，我可以悲叹不已；但是，他们赋予我生命，所以我也可以万分感激。

今天因为玫瑰的刺，我可以呜咽哭泣；但有刺的茎上有玫瑰花，所以我又可以欢欣庆贺。

今天因为自己缺少朋友，我可以哀伤悲痛；但我能去发掘新的感情，所以我又兴奋不已。

今天因为必须上班，我可以抱怨哭诉；但起码我还有工作可以去做，所以我可以高声欢呼。

今天因为必须做家务，我唉声叹气；但这是上帝赐予我的避风港，我又倍感荣耀。

今天伸展在我的面前，等着我去塑造，而我正是它的雕刻师，来赋予它某种形状。

今天是什么样，完全由我决定，今天怎样度过，由我来选择！

I woke up early today, excited over all I get to do before the clock strikes midnight. I have responsibilities to fulfill today. I am important.

My job is to choose what kind of day I am going to have.

Today I can complain because the weather is rainy or I can be thankful that the grass is getting watered for free.

Today I can feel sad that I don't have more money or I can be glad that my finances encourage me to plan my purchases wisely and guide me away from waste.

Today I can grumble about my health or I can rejoice that I am alive.

Today I can lament over all that my parents didn't give me when I was growing up or I can feel grateful that they allowed me to be born.

Today I can cry because roses have thorns or I can celebrate that thorns have roses.

Today I can mourn my lack of friends or I can excitedly embark upon a quest to discover new relationships.

Today I can whine because I have to go to work or I can shout for joy because I have a job to do.

Today I can murmur dejectedly because I have to do housework or I can feel honored because the Lord has provided shelter for my mind, body and soul.

Today stretches ahead of me, waiting to be shaped. And here I am, the sculptor who gets to do the shaping.

What today will be like is up to me. I get to choose what kind of day I will have!

快乐生活ABC

The ABCs of Living a Happy Life

佚名 / Anonymous

A

表示你承认并欣赏自己作为人的价值，你与生俱来便拥有自我意识、创造性的想象力、道德心、独立性、意志力和各种智能。

B

表示相信自己，相信自己有能力开发，并利用自身的潜能，使生活更有意义。

C

表示关爱自己与他人，关注自己对生活、学习、爱情和留下遗产的基本需求，并设身处地地为周围的人着想。

D

表示要有远大抱负，追求那些看似无法实现的梦想，这将指引你朝某一方向前进。

E

表示要对他人抱有同情心，理解他人的情绪和思想。

F

表示情趣，要享受生活，享受自己所做的事和自己做事的方式。

G

表示慷慨地将你的时间、积极的思想、善良的心和你能付出的所有都给予他人。

H

表示幸福，要对你的生活现状和所作所为感到幸福。

I

表示想象，要拓展你的思维，追逐梦想，寻找实现目标的途径。

J

表示喜悦，要把喜悦带给与你邂逅的人，以及与你一起生活和工作的人。

K

表示知识，要不断地学习，并将所学知识用于改善生活、改变社会。

L

表示关爱，无条件地去爱，不仅要在情绪和身体上，更要在精神上给予他人关爱。

M

表示动机、自律、自勉，同时也要激励他人进步。

N

表示友善，即使是对陌生人也要亲切友好。

O

表示开明，善于接纳他人、接受新思想以及荒谬却很有蛊惑力的想法。

P

表示耐心，要控制并调整自己，耐心地与天性同步。

Q

表示宁静，寻找宁静之地，进行内心反思，使自己活力四射。

R

表示尊重，要尊重种族、宗教、文化、信仰等价值观的差异性。

S

表示微笑，即使在绝望之时也要微笑面对。

T

表示信赖，要信赖自己、亲朋好友，以及其他人。

U

表示团结，与人和睦相处，重视家人、朋友、同事这样的统一团队。

V

表示胜利，不管你做什么，对微不足道的胜利都要加以赞赏并庆贺。

W

表示好奇，对人类、男人和女人以及自己和自然要满怀好奇心。

X

表示未知因素，探求自己及他人的独特之处，发现每个人独有的制胜因素。

Y

表示“是”，要敢于迎接所有积极的挑战和冒险。

Z

表示生活中的热情，无论做什么事都要满怀激情。

希望这些生活中的基本要素能引导你的生活。你也可以将这些用自己的话总结，让它们对你更有意义。

"A"is for acknowledging or appreciating your value as a person, gifted with endowments of self-awareness, creative imagination, conscience, independence, will and multipleintelligence.

"B"is for believing in yourself, that you have the ability to tap into your endowments to lead an effective, meaningful life.

"C"is for caring about yourself and people, taking care of your basic needs to live, learn, love and leave a legacy while caring for similar needs of other people around you.

"D"is for dreaming big dreams, to search for the wildest wishes that may seem impossible, but that begin to point you in certain directions.

"E"is for empathizing with people, understanding their feelings and their thinking.

"F"is for fun, allowing yourself to enjoy life, what you do and how you do things.

"G"is for giving generously your time, your positive thoughts, your kindness and whatever you can afford to bring to others.

"H"is for happiness, being happy with who you are and what you do in life.

"I"is for imagination, stretching your mind to search for dreams and solutions to achieve your goals.

"J"is for joy, bringing joy to people you meet, live with or work with.

"K"is for knowledge, always learning and using what you know for the betterment of life and society.

"L"is for love, loving unconditionally, not only emotionally or physically but spiritually.

"M"is for motivation, self-discipline and spurting yourself on as well as motivating people to excel.

"N"is for being nice, amiable and friendly even to strangers.

"O"is for openness, being open to people, new ideas and absurd but intriguing ideas.

"P"is for patience, to control oneself, to pace oneself and to follow certain steps in nature.

"Q"is for quiet, to find moments of quiet within yourself, to find a quiet spot to review, reflect and rejuvenate yourself.

"R"is for respect, to value diversity of races, religions, cultures, beliefs and values.

"S"is for smiling, the ability to smile freely even in moments of despair.

"T"is for trust, trusting yourself, your relatives, your friends and people.

"U"is for unity, in living peacefully with people and in valuing the input of a unified team of family, friends and colleagues.

"V"is for victory, recognizing and celebrating even the smallest victory in whatever you do.

"W"is for wonder, wondering about mankind, men and women, yourself and nature.

"X"is for the "X"factor, seeking the extra dimension in yourself and in people, finding the winning trait in each person.

"Y"is for saying "yes"to positive challenges and adventures.

"Z"is for zest in life, in whatever you set out to do.

May you be guided by these ABCs of life. Perhaps you can substitute your own words to make them more meaningful for you.

虽然有时我给读者一种悲观的错觉，但我从来不是一个本质悲观的人。

我更倾向于乐观，因为我非常严肃地看待生命。

悲观是浪费精力的情绪——是用以惩罚那些不知如何生活之人的。

行动才有幸福，每一股力量都是为了行动。

我始终觉得，无所事事比努力工作要痛苦得多。

快乐和热情是所有美德中最宝贵的。

逆境比顺境更能激发热情。

满足源于对周围环境的一种内在优越感。

我们常误认为展望未来意味着对未来的忧虑。满怀憧憬与愁眉紧锁一样容易。

几乎世上所有的罪恶和不幸都源于自私。我们很清楚这点，却仍执迷不悟地自私。

不能带来快乐的荣誉只能是一种遗憾。

乐观哲学

佚名 / Anonymous

ON

HAPPINESS

I have never been basically pessimistic, although I have appeared so to some readers.

I have taken life so seriously as to be disposed to optimism.

Pessimism is a waste of force—the penalty of one who doesn't know how to live.

Happiness is in action, and every power is intended for action.

I have always found that it's more painful to do nothing than something.

Of all the virtues, cheerfulness and enthusiasm are the most profitable.

Enthusiasm flourishes more often in adversity than it does in prosperity.

Contentment grows out of an inward superiority to our surroundings.

We fall into the mistake of supposing that to look forward must mean to look anxiously forward. It is just as easy to look forward with hope as with sadness.

The source of nearly all the evil and unhappiness of this world is selfishness. We know it; but we still keep on being selfish.

Fame without happiness is but a sorry at best.

让青春永驻的秘诀

How to Stay Young

佚名 / Anonymous

1．把那些无关紧要的数字抛至脑后，包括年龄、体重和身高。让医生去为它们操心，不然，你为什么要付钱给他们。

2. 只和快乐的人做朋友。那些满腹牢骚的人会让你情绪低落。

3. 不断学习，多学一些关于电脑、手工制作、园艺之类的技艺，什么都行。永远不要让大脑一片空白，空白的大脑是魔鬼的加工厂。

4. 在小事中寻找乐趣。

5. 开怀大笑，直到你笑得喘不过气来。

6. 偶尔让眼泪流下来，忍耐，悲痛，然后继续前进。漫漫人生，唯有我们自己是终身伴侣。活就应该活得精彩。

7. 让你所爱的一切围绕在身边，不管是家人，还是宠物、纪念品、音乐、植物、爱好，什么都行。

8. 珍爱你的健康。如果状况很好，保持它。如果不稳定，改善它。如果你无法改善，就寻求帮助。

9. 不要去可能让你悔恨的地方旅行。可以去逛逛街，去邻近的乡下，去国外，但可能让你悔恨的地方永远不要去。

10. 告诉你爱的人：你爱他们。不放过每一个表达爱的机会。

要永远记住：度量生命不是看寿命的长短，而是看一生中有过多少激动人心的时刻。

1.Throw out nonessential numbers. This includes age, weight and height. Let the doctor worry about them. That is why you pay him or her.

2.Keep only cheerful friends. The grouches pull you down.

3.Keep learning. Learn more about the computer, crafts, gardening, whatever. Never let the brain idle. An idle brain is the devil's workshop.

4.Enjoy the simple things.

5.Laugh often, long and loud. Laugh until you gasp for breath.

6.The tears happen. Endure, grieve, and move on. The only person who is with us our entire life is ourselves. Be ALIVE while you are alive.

7.Surround yourself with what you love, whether it's family, pets, keepsakes, music, plants, hobbies, whatever.

8.Cherish your health. If it is good, preserve it. If it is unstable, improve it. If it is beyond what you can improve, get help.

9.Don't take guilt trips. Take a trip to the mall , to the next country, to a foreign country, but not to where the guilt is.

10.Tell the people you love that you love them, at every opportunity.

And always remember: Life is not measured by the number of breaths we take, but by the moments that take our breath away.

享受生活中的每一刻
Experience Life

佚名 / Anonymous

我懂得什么是欲望、争斗、忧虑和绝望。我总是超负荷地工作。回望我的往昔生活，就如同战场一般，到处是梦想与希望的残垣断壁。这场不利于我的战争使我伤痕累累，甚至早衰。

我将生命之水一饮而尽，包括那些沉淀物，而她们只是浅尝了杯口的泡沫而已。我知道的东西她们永远也不能得知，我看到的事物，她们永远无法目睹。

女人的眼睛只有被泪水冲刷过，才会有更广阔的视野，才能在世界范围内有形同姐妹的朋友。

在充满艰辛曲折的社会大学中，我悟出了一条养尊处优的女人们无从学到的哲理。我学会了生活在今天，而不无聊地透支明天的烦恼。正是那种对未来的担忧使我们胆怯。因为经验告诉我：每当我非常害怕时，上天就会赋予我力量和智慧，于是，我不再胆怯。那些小小的烦恼再也无法影响我的行为——当你亲眼目睹了整座幸福的大厦在你面前轰然坍塌后，你就不会在意那些诸如仆人忘了在洗手盆下放垫子，厨师不慎把菜汤弄洒之类的琐事。

我学会了不对人们寄予过高的期望，因而，我仍能从那些并不真诚的朋友和爱搬弄是非的人那里获取快乐。另外，我还具有了幽默感，因为此前的许多事情都使我大喜大悲。如果一个女人在困难面前不再歇斯底里，仍能保持幽默，那就没有什么能伤害她了。

我不会为经历过的艰辛懊悔不已，因为在经历的过程中，我触摸到生活中的方方面面。它值得我为它付出一切。

I have known want and struggle and anxiety and despair. I have always had to work beyond the limits of my strength. As I look back upon my life, I see it as a battlefield strewn with the wrecks of dead dreams and broken hopes and shattered illusions—a battle in which I always fought with the odds tremendously against me, and which has left me scarred and bruised and maimed and old before my time.

I have drunk the cup of life down to its very dregs. They have only sipped the bubbles on top of it. I know things they will never know. I see things to which they are blind.

It is only the women whose eyes have been washed clear with tears who get the broad vision that makes them little sisters to all the world.

I have learned in the great University of Hard Knocks a philosophy that no woman who has had an easy life ever acquires. I have learned to live each day as it comes and not to borrow trouble by dreaming the tomorrow. It is the dark menace of the future that makes cowards of us. I put that dread from me because experience has taught me that when the time comes that I so fear, the strength and wisdom to meet it will be given me. Little annoyances no longer have the power to affect me. After you have seen your whole edifice of happiness topple and crash in ruins about you, it never matters to you again that a servant forgets to put the doilies under the finger bowls, or the cook spills the soup.

I have learned not to expect too much of people, and so I can still get happiness out of the friend who isn't quite true to me or the acquaintance who gossips. Above all, I have acquired a sense of humor, because there were so many things over which I had either to cry or laugh. And when a woman can joke over her troubles instead of having hysterics, nothing can ever hurt her much again.

I do not regret the hardships I have known, because through them I have touched life at every point I have lived. And it was worth the price I had to pay.

The Blue Day Book

你今天很郁闷吗

佚名 / Anonymous

人人都会有忧郁的时候。这些令人痛苦的日子，会让你感到恶心、烦躁、孤独、身心疲惫，你会觉得自己很渺小，总是被忽视，好像什么事情都做不好。你难以振作，重新开始仿佛是根本不可能的。忧郁的那几天，你会变成妄想狂，好像每个人都会吞掉你一样。你感觉失落和忧虑，你会疯狂地咬指甲，甚至在一眨眼的工夫就吃掉一大块巧克力蛋糕！忧郁、烦躁的日子里，你会觉得自己仿佛漂浮在悲伤的海洋里。你会毫无缘由地突然痛哭。最

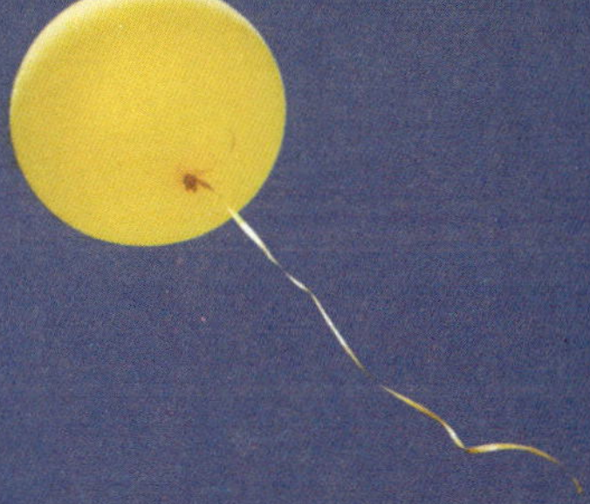

终，你感觉自己在生命中漫无目的地徘徊。你不知道自己还能坚持多久，只想大叫：“谁能一枪打死我！”一点儿小事就会带来忧郁、烦闷的一天。也许你一觉醒来，感觉上或看起来不是最好的自己，只是发现又有了新的皱纹，又胖了几斤，鼻子上长了个大痘痘。也许你忘记了约会对象的名字，或被刊登了一张令人尴尬的照片。也许你被人抛弃，离了婚，或被炒鱿鱼，被当众愚弄，被人起低贱的绰号，或每天都留着一头难看的旧发型，或许工作常让你碰壁。在巨大压力之下，你接替了别人的位置，老板对你百般刁难，办公室里的每个人都令你发狂。你也许会头疼欲裂，或摔跤、口臭、牙疼、放屁、嘴唇干裂或指甲长到肉里。无论是什么原因，你都深信，总是有人不喜欢你。哦，该怎么做，我该怎么办啊？

如果跟多数人一样，你躲起来，自欺欺人地认为所有的问题都会自动解决，那么你将会用尽余生回头张望，等着一次又一次重蹈覆辙。同时，你会变得脾气暴躁、愤世嫉俗，或变成可怜巴巴、涕泪横流的受害者。直到你沮丧地躺下

来，请求地面将你吞噬，或更糟糕的是，沉溺于比利·乔的歌曲中无法自拔。这真是疯狂，因为你的青春只有一次，绝不会有第二次。又有谁会知道拐角处还藏着什么奇迹呢？

当今世界上充满了令人惊奇的发现。有些事情你甚至无法想象。你可以分享那些有着令人迷醉的香气、味美绝伦的点心。你也许最终会拥有惊人的财富，甚至某天成为万人瞩目的超级巨星。听起来不错，是吧？但是等等，还有更多呢！你可以玩游戏或演奏乐器，还可以享受瑜伽、卡拉OK以及狂野、放荡不羁的舞蹈。但是所有的事之中，最美好的还是浪漫的爱情。这就意味着拥有长久的、梦幻般的凝视，耳边的甜言蜜语，无休无止的拥抱亲吻，一两个爱意绵绵的调皮咬痕，然后可能会发生任何事。这种幸福的感觉就好像滑入一个热气腾腾的泡泡浴池一样。那你怎样才能找到这种感觉呢？很简单。

首先要做的就是不要再逃避那些让你烦恼的事情，是时候去面对了。现在就让自己放松一下，深呼吸（用鼻子吸气，再用嘴呼出）。如果可以的话，试着沉思冥想，或散步清醒大脑。你必须放下感情的包袱，接受现实。试着换一个角度来看待问题，也许问题就出在你自己身上。如果真是如此，那就大大方方地说“对不起”（永远不要觉得太迟而不去做）。如果是他人做错了，那就站出来说：“那是不对的，我不会同意。”可以做得强硬一点儿（有时还可以发出嘘声）。为自己而骄傲，但不要忘了适度地自嘲（当你和积极的人交往时，这就非常容易了）。把生活中的每一天都当做生命的末日，因为它迟早会来的。不要害怕尝试超出自己能力的事情，要敢于承担巨大的风险，决不退缩，勇敢地走出这一步并努力去做好它。毕竟，生活不就是这样吗？

我也是这样想的。

Everybody has blue days. These are miserable days when you feel lousy, grumpy, lonely and utterly exhausted. Days when you feel small and insignificant, when everything seems just out of reach. You can't rise to the occasion. Just getting started seems impossible. On blue days you can become paranoid that everyone is out to get you.(This is not always such a bad thing) You feel frustrated and anxious, which can induce a nail-biting frenzy that can escalate into a triple-chocolate-mud—cake—eating frenzy in a blink of an eye! On blue days you feel like you're floating in an ocean of sadness. You're about to burst into tears at any moment and you don't even know why. Ultimately, you feel like you are wandering through life without purpose. You're not sure how much longer you can hang on and you feel like shouting, "Will someone please shoot me!"It doesn't take much to bring on a blue day. You might just wake up not feeling or looking your best, find some new wrinkles, put on a little weight, or get a huge pimple on your nose. You could forget your date's name or have an embarrassing photograph published. You might get dumped, divorced, or fired, make fool of yourself in public, be afflicted with a demeaning nickname, or just have a plain old bad-hair day. Maybe work is a pain in the butt. You're under major pressure to fill someone else's shoes, your boss is picking on you, and everyone in the office is driving you crazy. You might have a splitting headache, or a slipped disk, bad breath, a toothache, chronic gas, dry lips, or an ingrown toenail. Whatever the reason, you're convinced that someone up there doesn't like you. Oh what to do, what to do?

Well, if you're like most people, you'll hide behind a flimsy belief that everything will sort itself out. Then you will spend the rest of your life looking over your shoulder, waiting for everything to go wrong all over again. All the while becoming crusty and cynical or a pathetic, sniveling victim. Until you get so depressed that you lie down and beg the earth to swallow you up or, even worse, become addicted to Billy Joel songs. This is crazy, because you're only young once and you're never old twice. Who knows what fantastic things are in store just around the corner?

After all, the world is full of amazing discoveries, things you can't even imagine now. There are delicious, happy sniffs and scrumptious snacks to share. Hey, you might end up fabulously rich or even become a huge superstar (one day). Sounds good, doesn't it? But wait, there's more!There are handstands, and games to play and yoga and karaoke and wild, crazy, bohemian dancing. But best of all, there's romance. Which means long dreamy stares, whispering sweet nothings, cuddles, smooches, more smooches and even more smooches, a frisky love bite or two, and then, well, anything goes. So how can you find that blissful "just sliding into a hot bubble bath"kind of feeling? It's easy.

First, stop slinking away from all those nagging issues. It's time to face the music. Now just relax. Take some deep breaths.(in through the nose and out through the mouth.) Try to meditate if you can. Or go for a walk to clear your head. Accept the fact that you'll have to let go of some emotional baggage. Try seeing things from a different perspective. Maybe you're actually the one at fault.

If that's the case, be big enough to say you're sorry (it is never too late to do this). If someone else is doing the wrong thing, stand up and say, "That's not right and I won't stand for it!"It's OK to be forceful (It's really okay to blow raspberries). Be proud of who you are, but don't lose the ability to laugh at yourself(This is a lot easier when you associate with positive people). Live every day as if it were your last, because one day it will be. Don't be afraid to bite off more than you can chew. Take big risks. Never hang back. Get out there and go for it. After all, isn't that what life is all about?

I think so too.

HAPPINESS IS A STIMULUS

用快乐激发出更多的快乐

佚名 / Anonymous

很多人都找到了令自己快乐的源泉——有些人全身心地投入工作；有些人沉湎于吸毒和酗酒；还有数不清的人，从名贵汽车、异国情调的度假小屋以及其他一些流行“玩具”中寻找到了快乐。他们的努力大多基于一个共同的事实：人们在寻找永恒的快乐源泉。

但我认为，很多人与快乐无缘。因为他们错误地理解了寻找快乐的过程。

现在，有些人认为名贵汽车、高薪工作和爱情都是刺激物，而快乐就是刺激的结果。这种想法让我们觉得：“当我拥有……时，我才会快乐。”

但我发现，事实恰好相反。我相信快乐也是一种刺激物，而它作为刺激的结果，是生活给那些真正快乐的人的馈赠。我们快乐时，就会在工作上取得更多的成功；我们快乐时，就会有融洽的人际关系，也会得到爱情的垂青；我们快乐时，就会很自然地善待自己，关注自身健康。快乐并不是刺激的结果，而是一种刺激物。

快乐是我们每天在生活中作出的有意识的选择。不知为何，我认为，许多人多数时候都选择让自己痛苦、沮丧和恼怒。快乐并不是得到自己想要的东西之后的感觉——我们往往是在选择快乐之后，才会得到自己想要的东西。

Many have sought a variety of sources for their feeling of happiness. Some have put their heart and efforts into their work. Too many turned to drugs and alcohol. Untold numbers have looked for it in the possession of expensive cars, exotic vacation hoes, and other popular "toys". Most of their efforts have a root in one common fact that people are looking for a lasting source of happiness.

Unfortunately, I believe that happiness evades many because they misunderstand the process and journey of finding it.

Today, some people think that an expensive car is stimulus. Happiness is a response. A great paying job is stimulus. Happiness is a response. A loving relationship is stimulus. Happiness is a response. This belief leaves us thinking and feeling: "I'll be happy when ..."

It has been my finding that actually the opposite is true. I believe that happiness is a stimulus and response is what life brings to those who are truly happy. When we are happy, we tend to have more success in our work. When we are happy, people want to be around us and enjoy loving relationships. When we are happy, we more naturally take better care of our bodies and enjoy good health. Happiness is not a response—rather, it is a stimulus.

Happiness is a conscious choice we make every day of our lives. For unknown reasons to me, many choose to be miserable, frustrated and angry most of the time. Happiness is not something that happens to us after we get something we want—we usually get things we want after we choose to be happy.

一个大学生曾和我说："我不需要快乐——我只要成功。"

这是一个奇怪的思想对比。她不需要快乐——"只要成功"。她将这两者对立起来。

对学生而言，今天的言就是明天的行。他们所说的话很具有代表性，每个人都会努力奋斗，只是这种努力往往不易觉察。

记得上大学时，校报上有一篇文章的标题是这样的：《为什么我们不快乐》。这个标题表明：我们感到快乐在缺失。然而，至少我们仍在寻找。像那个追求成功的学生一样，许多人宁愿放弃快乐，这是为什么呢？

远离忧虑才能获取快乐　Don't Let Happiness Run Away From Us

为了确保周一的工作进度，我在周日也常常加班。这实际上是提前对未来一周的工作感到焦虑——担心会发生意想不到的麻烦，或觉得自己在某些方面做不好。但我通常在正常上班的日子做得很不错。我担心的很多事从未发生过。

快乐自有其道德基础。快乐的完整性让我们不得不考虑自己应该做什么样的人。当然，一些不怎么光彩的行为也会衍生快乐。但是，要想体验快乐，我们就得付出更多。正是快乐，让我们体会到事物的可贵之处。

真正的快乐需要作出选择，这些选择可以养成习惯，从而形成性格。这是我们无法推脱的。

因此，获取真正快乐的首要一步就是减少忧虑——这个关键的第一步能让我们远离忧虑。它要求我们勇于接受毫无预想的一切，坦然面对生活中的不完美。

◀ 佚名 / Anonymous

A college student once told me: "I don't need to be happy—just successful."

It's an odd juxtaposition. She needn't be happy— "just successful". She places one in opposition to the other.

Students are today's expressions of tomorrow's practices. Their words can be the visible signs of the less visible struggles encountered by us all.

I have a memory from my own undergraduate years of a headline in my campus newspaper: Why Aren't We Happy?As the headline suggests, we fell short of leading joyful lives. Yet, at least happiness was still on the agenda. What underlies the tendency of many of us, like my success-seeking student, to give up genuinely trying?

I've often failed to enjoy Sunday because of my schedule on Monday. At bottom, it was simply anticipatory anxiety over the work of the week ahead—fear that there would be unexpected complications or that I would fail to measure up in some way. Usually, when Monday came, I did quite well. Much of what I worried about never happened.

Joy has its own moral underpinning. There's a completeness to joy that does not allow us to exclude our sense of the person we should be. Pleasure is certainly possible in less-than-honorable actions. But the experience of joy requires more; it is pleasure taken in worthy things.

True joy requires choices that develop into habits that evolve into character. And that's work we can't delegate.

The essential first step is trying to live a less fearful life—one that avoids collapsing life's possibilities before exploring them. It entails welcoming uncertainty and comfortable incompleteness.

享受阳光

Time for Sunshine

▶ 佚名 / Anonymous

经过了漫长的冬季，春天总会让你有截然不同的感觉。当你的生活被撒上一层阳光时，你感觉有多爽？阳光对我们的精神究竟有怎样的影响？阳光能赋予我们安慰、乐观和自信，当然也少不了微笑。设想一下，如果一整年我们都是如此积极，那该多好！

假如你真想拥有这样的生活，是完全可能的。但是为了拥有这样快乐的生活状态，我们必须让阳光发自内心，源自心灵、头脑和灵魂。我确信大部分正在读这篇文章的人都会说：“是啊，说着容易，做着难！”对此，我们该如何回答呢？嗯，最后的决定权在你的手中。假如你确实那样认为，你的生活就会反映出你的那种态度！

为了让“阳光”——或者说是“光明”——成为我们生命的组成部分，我们需要审视自己的思想、言辞以及行为，避免现实中

的自己和自己真正想要在生活中创造出的东西产生矛盾，这一点尤其重要。要审视自己的想法，彻底弄清自己头脑中有多少关于自己和周围其他人的消极想法，注意自己是不是讲了许多别人的闲话。一旦你认识到这一点，你就会明白其实这些都源自你自身的嫉妒和不安全感。

你还应该认真地审视自己的“动机”。有多少人为别人做事而不图回报？或许你期待的不一定是物质或身体上的回报，对认可或感谢的期待完全可以作为你的“动机”。好好想想吧！我们或许不会一直关注言行和思想背后的真正动机，因为我们中的许多人并没有认识到动机在创造生活中的力量和影响。

总结所有这些因素，好像我们中的大多数人都在内心创造出了一个怪物，我们仅仅是在谈论、思考，对帮助别人却没有怀着适当的动机去表露真心。一切都源于一种“否定”的态度，而当关系到给生活带来更为明亮的“阳光”时，这些根本不会对我们有所帮助。假如你把一切消极的态度都放在一只手中，并在另一只手中权衡你对“阳光”的需要，你就会明白，这些因素相互之间到底有多么矛盾。

勇敢些吧，在这个春天改变你的模式和习惯。唯有这样，你才能让真正的阳光从心底放射，让阳光照进你的生活，也照进你周围人的生活。

Having spring around makes you feel different after such a long winter journey. How well do you feel when you have a little bit of sunshine in your life? What effect does it have on our psyche? The power of sunshine brings us a lot of comfort, optimism, self-confidence and of course a smile. Imagine how great it would be if we were so positive all year round!

Living like this is possible if you really think about it. In order to exist in such a state of happiness though, we must have sunshine radiating from within ourselves, shining from our hearts, our minds and from our souls. I bet many of you are reading this now and saying, "Yeah, that is easier said than done!"And what do we say to that? Well, in the end that's your choice, and if you think that way then your own life will reflect that attitude of yours!

In order to make "sunshine"or rather, "light"a part of our being, it is so important that you watch your thoughts, your words and your actions so that you do not contradict what you really feel you'd like to create in your own life. Watch your thoughts and really become aware of how many negative thoughts pass through your mind about yourself and other people around you. Watch to see how often you gossip about other people, and when you become aware of it you will see how often it is actually attached with feelings of jealousy, envy and insecurity about yourself.

You should also take a close look at your "intention". How many of you do something for another person without expecting to receive something in return? It might not even have to be a material or physical thing you expect; expecting recognition or acknowledgement for what you have done is enough to create conditions on your intention. Think about it! We may not always pay attention to what our true intentions are behind our words, thoughts and actions because many of us are not aware of the power and effect they have when it comes to creating our lives.

Putting all of these together, it seems that most of us are creating monsters inside of us just by simply talking, thinking and not putting our heart out with the right intention towards helping someone else. All of these things are born from a "negative"attitude and will not help us in any way at all when it comes to bringing a brighter "sunshine"into our lives. If you took all your negative attitudes in one hand and measured your need to feel "sunshine"in the other, you would see how both these elements really contradict each other.

Be brave and break your patterns and your habits this spring, and by doing so you will allow the true sunshine to take place by radiating out from your heart and into your life and the lives of the people who are around you!

佚名 / Anonymous

Free to Soar

放飞心灵

一个春风拂面的日子，一群年轻人正在放风筝。天空中满是各种颜色、形状和大小的风筝，犹如穿梭飞舞着的漂亮鸟儿。强劲有力的风吹着风筝，牵引线控制着它们。

风筝并不是随风而去，而是迎风飘往高处。风的劲吹使它们摇晃着、拉扯着，但牵引线和笨重的尾翼让它们始终处于控制之中。它们挣扎着、抖动着，似乎在说："放开我！放开我！我要自由！"就是在与牵引线抗争之时，它们也依然优雅地飞翔着。终于，其中一只风筝成功地挣脱了线的束缚，它好像在说：**"终于自由了，终于可以随风自由飞翔了。"**

然而，没有束缚的自由让它完全处于风的无情摆布之下。它笨拙地坠落到地面，落在一堆乱草之中，线也缠在一丛枯死的灌木上了。"终于自由了"——自由到无力地躺在泥土中，自由到无助地任由风吹得满地跑，自由到撞到第一个障碍物就搁浅，毫无生气可言。

有时候，我们与风筝是多么相似啊！上天让我们经历逆境，体验束缚，并定下规则约束我们，让我们从中成长起来，获得人生所需的力量。逆风而行时，束缚是不可或缺的。有些人强硬地抵制这些规则，那就永远也飞不到本可以达到的高度。只遵从部分规则，我们绝不可能飞得很高。

每个人都飞到高处吧，同时也要认识到——某些令人恼怒的约束，实际上是帮助我们攀升、飞跃和达到目标的强大力量。

One windy spring day, I observed young people having fun using the wind to fly their kites. Multicolored creations of varying shapes and sizes filled the skies like beautiful birds darting and dancing. As the strong winds gusted against the kites, a string kept them in check.

Instead of blowing away with the wind, they arose against it to achieve great heights. They shook and pulled, but the restraining string and the cumbersome tail kept them in tow, facing upward and against the wind. As the kites struggled and trembled against the string, they seemed to say, "Let me go! Let me go! I want to be free!"They soared beautifully even as they fought the restriction of the string. Finally, one of the kites succeeded in breaking loose. "Free at last,"it seemed to say. "Free to fly with the wind."

Yet freedom from restraint simply put it at the mercy of an unsympathetic breeze. It fluttered ungracefully to the ground and landed in a tangled mass of weeds and string against a dead bush. "Free at last", free to lie powerless in the dirt, to be blown helplessly along the ground, and to lodge lifeless against the first obstruction.

How much like kites we sometimes are. Heaven gives us adversity and restrictions, rules to follow from which we can grow and gain strength. Restraint is a necessary counterpart to the winds of opposition. Some of us tug at the rules so hard that we never soar to reach the heights we might have obtained. We keep part of the commandment and never rise high enough to get our tails off the ground.

Let us each rise to the great heights, recognizing that some of the restraints that we may chafe under are actually the steadying force that helps us ascend and achieve.

清晨最美好的愿望

A MORNING WISH

佚名 / Anonymous

朝阳在新的一天冉冉升起。我期望这一天带给我什么呢？希望不是任何让世界或他人更贫穷的东西，不是任何损害别人的东西，而是那些到来、经过或者聚集力量时，不会阻止我前进并且能触动我心灵的东西。

我盼望这一天会带来一些知心的朋友，希望我们的友谊天长地久；我也希望这一天能够给我带来一份真正有价值的工作。

我盼望这一天会带给我无畏远行的胸怀，纵然旅途中没有光明在闪耀；我还盼望这一天会带给我善解人意之心。

我盼望这一天会让我看到永久屹立的山冈，看到一望无际的蓝色海洋，看到人类的双手创造出的美丽事物。

我盼望这一天会带给我幽默感、笑的力量和无事可做的短暂悠闲。

这天早上，我渴望短暂宁静的冥想。

The sun is just rising in the morning of another day. What can I wish that this day may bring me? Nothing that shall make the world or others poorer, nothing at the expense of other men; but just those few things which in their coming do not stop me but touch me rather, as they pass and gather strength.

I wish that this day could bring me a few friends, who understand me, and yet remain my friends; I also wish that this day could bring me a work to do which has real value.

I wish that this day could bring me a mind unafraid to travel, even though the trail be not blazed, and I wish that this day could bring me an understanding heart.

I wish that this day could bring me a sight of the eternal hills, and the blue sea stretching to the horizon, and of something beautiful which the hands of men have made.

I wish that this day could bring me a sense of humor, and the power to laugh, a little leisure with nothing to do.

And I crave for a few moments of quiet, silent meditation in the morning of this day.

祈祷之手

The Praying Hands

佚名 / Anonymous

早在15世纪时，纽伦堡附近的一个小村庄里，有一个家庭有18个孩子。18个！为了解决这个大家庭的温饱，身为金匠的一家之主的父亲每天要工作近18个小时，而且，还得在邻居那找些杂活做。

尽管他们的处境很困窘，但阿尔布雷希特?丢勒的两个儿子阿尔布雷希特和阿尔贝特，依然拥有梦想。他们都想继续发展自己的艺术才能，但也都清楚地意识到他们的父亲甚至不可能供他们中的任何一个去纽伦堡上美术学院。

无数个夜晚，他们挤在床头彻夜长谈。最后，两兄弟终于达成一个协议——掷硬币，谁输了，谁就去附近的矿井，用挣来的钱供他的兄弟上美术学院。然后，等赢的那个完成四年的学业后，就支持另一个上学，可以用卖画的钱，或者，如有必要，还要当矿工。

一个星期天的早晨，做完礼拜后，他们掷了硬币。阿尔布雷希特·丢勒赢了，他去了纽伦堡。阿尔贝特则下到危险的矿井里，整整四年供他的兄弟上学。他的兄弟很快轰动了美术学院，阿尔布雷希特的蚀刻画、木版画和油画甚至远远超过了他的一些教授的水平。快要毕业时，他已经靠替人作画获得了一笔可观的收入。

当这个年轻的画家回到故乡，丢勒一家在自家门口的草坪上，举办宴席以庆祝阿尔布雷希特衣锦还乡。难忘的宴席持续进行了很长时间，汇成了歌声和欢笑声的海洋。阿尔布雷希特从荣耀的座位上站起来，向他敬爱的兄弟敬酒，感谢他为自己作出的牺牲，使自己梦想成真。他最后说道："现在，阿尔贝特，我可敬的兄弟，轮到你去上学了。你可以去纽伦堡追逐你的梦想了，我会照顾你的。"

所有的人都迫切地转向远在桌角的阿尔贝特，他坐在那儿，眼泪滑过他苍白的面孔，他的头低垂着，不停地摇晃。他呜咽着一遍又一遍地说："不……不……不……不。"

最终，阿尔贝特站起来，擦掉脸上的泪，扫视着长桌旁亲人们的面庞。然后，他举起手放到右脸颊旁，轻声说道：“不，兄弟，我不能去纽伦堡了，这对我来说，太晚了。在矿井的四年，看看我的手被折磨成什么样了！手上的每一根骨头至少折过一次。最近，我的右手患了严重的关节炎，我甚至都不能举起酒杯来回敬你，更别说拿笔或刷在纸上画细腻的线条了。不用了，兄弟，这对我太晚了。”

450多年过去了，如今，全世界各大博物馆里都珍藏着阿尔布雷希特·丢勒成千上万的杰作。不过，你也许和大多数人一样，可能只熟悉他的一幅作品，也可能不仅是熟悉，你家里或办公室里也许就挂着这幅画的复制品。

为了向阿尔贝特作出的牺牲表示敬意，阿尔布雷希特·丢勒将他兄弟饱经摧残的手指和掌心，细致入微地描绘了下来，干枯的手指伸向天空。他将这幅力作简单地命名为《手》，全世界很快为之轰动，人们将这爱的献礼重新命名为《祈祷之手》。

下次看到这幅感人的画作的复制品时，你要多留心。如果需要，就让它时刻提醒你：没有人能单枪匹马取得成功！

Back in the Fifteenth Century, in a tiny village near Nuremberg, lived a family with eighteen children. Eighteen! In order merely to keep food on the table for this mob, the father and head of the household, a goldsmith by profession, worked almost eighteen hours a day at his trade and any other paying chore he could find in the neighborhood.

Despite their seemingly hopeless condition, two of Albrecht Durer the Elder's children, Albrecht and Albert, had a dream. They both wanted to pursue their talent for art, but they knew full well that their father would never be financially able to send either of them to Nuremberg to study at the academy.

After many long discussions at night in their crowded bed, the two boys finally worked out a pact. They would toss a coin. The loser would go down into the nearby mines and, with his earnings, support his brother while he attended the academy. Then, when the brother who won the toss completed his studies, in four years, he would support the other brother at the academy, either with sales of his artwork or, if necessary, also by laboring in the mines.

They tossed a coin on a Sunday morning after church. Albrecht Durer won the toss and went off to Nuremberg. Albert went down into the dangerous mines and, for the next four years, financed his brother, whose work at the academy was almost an immediate sensation. Albrecht's etchings, his woodcuts, and his oils were far better than those of most of his professors, and by the time he graduated, he was beginning to earn considerable fees for his commissioned works.

When the young artist returned to his village, the Durer family held a festive dinner on their lawn to celebrate Albrecht's triumphant home-coming. After a long and memorable meal, punctuated with music and laughter, Albrecht rose from his honored position at the head of the table to drink a toast to his beloved brother for the years of sacrifice that had enabled Albrecht to fulfill his ambition. His closing words were, "And now, Albert, blessed brother of mine, now it is your turn. Now you can go to Nuremberg to pursue your dream, and I will take care of you."

All heads turned in eager expectation to the far end of the table where Albert sat, tears streaming down his pale face, shaking his lowered head from side to side while he sobbed and repeated over and over, "No... no... no... no."

Finally, Albert rose and wiped the tears from his cheeks. He glanced down the long table at the faces he loved, and then, holding his hands close to his right cheek, he said softly, "No, brother. I cannot go to Nuremberg. It is too late for me. Look, what four years in the mines have done to my hands! The bones in every finger have been smashed at least once, and lately I have been suffering from arthritis so badly in my right hand that I cannot even hold a glass to return your toast, much less make delicate lines on parchment or canvas with a pen or a brush.

No, my brother... for me it is too late."

More than 450 years have passed. By now, Albrecht Durer's hundreds of masterful portraits hang in every great museum in the world, but the odds are great that you, like most people, are familiar with only one of Albrecht Durer's works. More than merely being familiar with it, you very well may have a reproduction hanging in your home or office.

To pay homage to Albert for all that he had sacrificed, Albrecht Durer painstakingly drew his brother's abused hands with palms together and thin fingers stretched skyward. He called his powerful drawing simply Hands, but the entire world almost immediately opened their hearts to his great masterpiece and renamed his tribute of love The Praying Hands.

The next time you see a copy of that touching creation, take a second look. Let it be your reminder, if you still need one, that no one—no one—ever makes it alone!

让轻松和快乐与你随行

Go Easy and Enjoy Yourself in Harmony

佚名 / Anonymous

人在旅途，难免有不安与困惑伴你同行。不管怎样，你都要继续自己的人生之旅。人生之旅的走法因人而异。有的人步履匆忙，心急意切。他们只关注及时到达目的地，根本无暇观赏路边的风景。可路途漫漫，终点何在呢？有的人像游客，不紧不慢，时而停下来观花开花落，看云卷云舒，时而逆风而行，冒雨而进。他们不会苦恼，因为烦躁与苦恼已从敞开的胸怀中溜走。

狭小的工作场所，拥挤的居住空间，局限的社交圈子——人们对这一成不变的单调越来越不满。然而，如果一个人随遇而安，总能找到安宁与舒适。浩渺的大千世界，一个人只能占据其中微小的一隅。然而，比海洋更宽广的是天空，比天空更宽广的是人的心灵，因为有一对想象的翅膀进驻于这小小的心灵，它可以尽情地飞翔。

当一个人最终得到他想要的东西时，却发现自己已经失去了太多太多，或许他会得不偿失。

人生旅途上，一些人带着追名逐利的疲乏之心奋力前行；另一些人则自在逍遥地与自然和谐相处，享受人生。

To go on a journey is often worrisome, but so long as one lives he proceeds on his life's journey. Different people go along differently. Some take hasty steps in anxiety. Obsessed with reaching the next goal in time, they spare no time for sight-seeing along the way, nor do they have a clear view where their long roads end. Others travel leisurely like tourists. They would take time off now and then for a look at blooming flowers or fallen petals. They would stop to admire clouds gathering and dispersing. Even when they go against the wind or are caught in the rain, they never get annoyed, for worries slip off their minds as if from an open net.

Cramped is one's workplace. Narrow is one's residenceand small is the social circle one moves about—such limitedness in space entail lack of variety which is the source of some people's complaint. But a person is always able to find peace and comfort if he takes things as they are. Compared with the vastness of the universe it is only a tiny spot one occupies on earth. However, though larger than the ocean is the sky, even larger is the human mind, for in it imagination would come and go on the wing without limitations.

One may eventually win what he has set his mind to, only to find that he has lost quite a lot. Perhaps what he loses is even better than what he gains.

On one's journey of life some people hurry on with a heavy heart in pursuitof fame and wealth while others go easy and enjoy themselves in harmony with nature.

选择乐观

CHOOSE OPTIMISM

佚名 / Anonymous

如果你预料某事会很糟糕，那么它很可能真会这样。悲观的想法一般都能实现。反过来，这个原理同样成立。如果你料想会好运连连，通常也会这样！乐观和成功之间似乎有一种天然的因果关系。

乐观和悲观都是强大的力量，我们塑造和展望未来，都必须从中作出选择。每个人的生命中都有太多的幸运或灾难：充满着忧伤和快乐、无限的喜悦和痛苦——不论我们是悲观还是乐观，都有充分的理由。我们可以选择哭或笑、祝福或诅咒。这是我们的决定：选择用什么样的眼光来看待人生？是在希望中昂首阔步，还是在绝望中低头长叹？

我喜欢展望未来。我选择关注积极面，忽视消极面。我是乐观主义者，更多的是因为我的选择，而非天性。当然，我知道，生命中总存在着悲伤。现在，我已经70多岁了，经历过太多灾难。但是，当一切尘埃落定，我发现生命中的美好远多于丑恶。

乐观的态度并非奢侈品，而是一种必需。你看待生活的方式决定了你如何去感受、去表现，以及你与他人如何相处。相反地，消极的思想、态度和预想也决定了这些，它们成为一种能自我实现的预言。悲观会制造一种阴沉的生活，没有人愿意活在其中。

几年前，我开车去一个加油站加油。那天天气很晴朗，我心情很好。当我进站付油费时，服务员对我说："你感觉怎么样啊？"这个问题有些莫名其妙，但我感觉很好，也这样跟他说了。"你脸色不大好。"他说。我十分惊讶，于是，我告诉他，我确实感觉不错，但已不再信心十足了。他毫不犹豫地继续说我的脸色如何不好，连皮肤都发黄了。

我心神不宁地离开加油站，开了一个街区后，我把车停在路边，照着镜子看看自己的脸。我怎么了？是不是得黄疸病了？一切都正常吗？回到家时，我开始想吐了，我的肝脏是不是出了问题？我不会染上什么怪病了吧？

我再次去那个加油站时，又感觉不错了，也明白了究竟是怎么一回事。这个地方最近涂了一种明亮、胆汁质的黄色油漆，灯光反射在墙壁上，让里面的人看起来像是得了肝炎。我想，不知道有多少人也有过类似的经历呢！我的心情因为与一个完全陌生的人短暂交谈，整整改变了一天。他告诉我，我看起来像生病了，而后不久，我真的感觉不舒服。这个消极的观点，深刻地影响了我的感受和行为。

唯一比消极更具力量的是一个积极的肯定，一句乐观和希望的言辞。最让我欣慰的是，我是在一个有着乐观主义光荣传统的国度里成长的。当整体文化积极向上时，再难以置信的事也能完成。当世界看起来充满希望时，人们就会在这个积极的场所努力向上，并获得成功。

乐观并不需要变得幼稚，我们可以在成为乐观者的同时，仍意识到问题的存在，有些甚至难以解决。但是，乐观使解决问题的态度有所不同！乐观会使我们把注意力从消极转到积极的、建设性的思考上。如果你是一个乐观者，会更关心问题的解决，而不是毫无价值地怨天尤人。事实上，如果没有乐观主义精神，一些现存的巨大问题，如贫穷，就毫无希望解决。它需要一个梦想家——一个拥有绝对乐观、矢志不渝、坚定信念的人——来解决这个巨大的问题。乐观，或是悲观，在于你的选择。

If you expect something to turn out badly, it probably will. Pessimism is seldom disappointed. But the same principle also works in reverse. If you expect good things to happen, they usually do! There seems to be a natural cause-and-effect relationship between optimism and success.

Optimism and pessimism are both powerful forces, and each of us must choose which we want to shape our outlook and our expectations. There is enough good and bad in everyone's life—ample sorrow and happiness, sufficient joy and pain—to find a rational basis for either optimism or pessimism. We can choose to laugh or cry, bless or curse. It's our decision: From which perspective do we want to view life? Will we look up in hope or down in despair?

I believe in the upward look. I choose to highlight the positive and slip right over the negative. I am an optimist by choice as much as by nature. Sure, I know that sorrow exists. I am in my 70s now, and I've lived through more than one crisis. But when all is said and done, I find that the good in life far outweighs the bad.

An optimistic attitude is not a luxury; it's a necessity. The way you look at life will determine how you feel, how you perform, and how well you will get along with other people. Conversely, negative thoughts, attitudes, and expectations feed on themselves; they become a self-fulfilling prophecy. Pessimism creates a dismal place where no one wants to live.

Years ago, I drove into a service station to get some gas. It was a beautiful day, and I was feeling great. As I walked into the station to pay for the gas, the attendant said to me, "How do you feel?"That seemed like an odd question, but I felt fine and told him so. "You don't look well,"he replied. This took me completely by surprise. A little less confidently, I told him that I had never felt better. Without hesitation, he continued to tell me how bad I looked and that my skin appeared yellow.

By the time I left the service station, I was feeling a little uneasy. About a block away, I pulled over to the side of the road to look at my face in the mirror. How did I feel? Was I jaundiced? Was everything all right? By the time I got home, I was beginning to feel a little queasy. Did I have a bad liver? Had I picked up some rare disease?

The next time I went into that gas station, feeling fine again, I figured out what had happened. The place had recently been painted a bright, bilious yellow, and the light reflecting off the walls made everyone inside look as though they had hepatitis! I wondered how many other folks had reacted the way I did. I had let one short conversation with a total stranger change my attitude for an entire day. He told me I looked sick, and before long, I was actually feeling sick. That single negative observation had a profound effect on the way I felt and acted.

The only thing more powerful than negativism is a positive affirmation, a word of optimism and hope. One of the things I am most thankful for is the fact that I have grown up in a nation with a grand tradition of optimism. When a whole culture adopts an upward look, incredible things can be accomplished. When the world is seen as a hopeful, positive place, people are empowered to attempt and to achieve.

Optimism doesn't need to be naive. We can be an optimist and still recognize that problems exist and that some of them are not dealt with easily. But what a difference optimism makes in the attitude of the problem solver! Optimism diverts our attention away from negativism and channels it into positive, constructive thinking. When you're an optimist, you're more concerned with problem-solving than with useless carping about issues. In fact, without optimism, issues as big and ongoing as poverty have no hope of solution. It takes a dreamer—someone with hopelessly optimistic ideas, great persistence, and unlimited confidence—to tackle a problem that big. It's your choice.

幸福最好

佚名 / Anonymous

HAPPINESS IS BETTER

我们努力想让子女生活得更好，最终却事与愿违。对我的孙儿们，我知道怎么做才会更好。

我很想让他们知道，兄长传给我的旧衣服，小时候吃过的家里自制的冰淇淋，以及吃剩的肉糕。我的确很想讲给他们听。

我的宝贝孙子，我希望你在遭遇失败后懂得谦逊，也希望你能诚实，即使没有人注意你。

我希望你能学会整理床铺，修剪草坪，清洗汽车，也希望当你满16岁时，没有人送你新轿车。

我希望你能有幸目睹一次牛犊出生的过程，或者在你不得不为老狗送终时有朋友陪伴。

我希望你能为自己的信仰与别人打得鼻青脸肿。

我希望你能和弟弟分享同一间卧室——即使你在卧室中间画一条分界线也无所谓。当弟弟因为害怕要钻进你的被窝时，我希望你能收留他。

还有，当你要去看迪斯尼电影，而弟

弟想跟你一起去时，我希望你能带上他。

我希望你能与朋友们一起爬山，如果这项运动在你生活的城市没有任何危险。

如果你想要一把弹弓，我希望你父亲能教你自己制作，而不是给你买把现成的。我还希望你学会挖泥巴和读书；而当你学会使用电脑时，也应该学会加减法的心算。

我希望吸烟的人在你面前吞云吐雾时，你会感到厌烦。我不介意你喝一次啤酒，但我希望你不会喜欢上它。如果有朋友请你吸含大麻的香烟或其他毒品，我希望你能清醒地认识到他并不是你的朋友。

我当然希望你能抽时间陪爷爷坐在门廊上聊天，或陪叔叔钓鱼。

如果你把棒球扔到邻居的窗户上，我希望你的母亲会责罚你。如果你把以自己的手为原型做成的石膏模型送给母亲，我希望她会拥抱你、亲吻你。

我希望你能饱尝岁月的艰辛、挫折与失望，并希望你努力工作，幸福快乐。

We tried so hard to make things better for our kids that we made them worse. For my grandchildren, I'd know better.

I'd really like for them to know about hand-me-down clothes and homemade ice cream and leftover meat loaf. I really would.

My cherished grandson, I hope you learn humility by surviving failure and that you learn to be honest even when no one is looking.

I hope you learn to make your bed and mow the lawn and wash the car and I hope nobody gives you a brand-new car when you are sixteen.

It will be good if at least one time you can see a baby calf born, and you have a good friend to be with you if you ever have to put your old dog to sleep.

I hope you get a black eye fighting for something you believe in.

I hope you have to share a bedroom with your younger brother. And it is all right to draw a line down the middle of the room, but when he wants to crawl under the covers with you because he's scared, I hope you'll let him.

And when you want to see a Disney movie and your kid brother wants to tag along, I hope you take him.

I hope you have to walk up hill with your friends and that you live in a town where you can do it safely.

If you want a slingshot, I hope your father teaches you how to make one instead of buying one. I hope you learn to dig in the dirt and read books, and when you learn to use computers, you also learn how to add and subtractin your head.

I hope you get sick when someone blows smoke in your face. I don't care if you try beer once, but I hope you won't like it. And if a friend offers you a joint or any drugs, I hope you are smart enough to realize that person is not your friend.

I sure hope you make time to sit on a porch with your grandpa or go fishing with your uncle.

I hope your mother punishes you when you throw a baseball through a neighbor's window, and that she hugs you and kisses you when you give her a plaster of pared mold of your hand.

These things I wish for you—tough times and disappointment, hard work and happiness.

佚名 / Anonymous

Be Grateful to Life

常怀感恩之心

美国总统罗斯福的家曾经失窃，财物损失严重。朋友闻此消息，就写信安慰他，劝他不必把这件事放在心上。罗斯福总统很快回信说："亲爱的朋友，谢谢你来信安慰我，我一切都很好。我想我应该感谢上帝，因为：第一，我损失的只是财物，人却毫发未损；第二，我只损失了部分财物，而非所有财产；第三，最幸运的是，做小偷的是那个人，而不是我……"

对任何人来说，家中失窃绝非幸事。但是，罗斯福总统却能找到三个感恩的理由。这个故事告诉我们：生活中，我们应该学会感恩。

感恩是一项重要的处世哲学，是生活的大智慧。人生在世，不可能事事顺通。对于各种失败和不幸，我们要豁达大度，勇敢地面对失败和不幸，并想办法解决。面对困难，我们是懊恼抱怨、沮丧气馁、陷入绝望，还是对生活满怀感恩之心，跌倒后再爬起来呢？英国著名作家威廉·萨克雷说过：“生活是一面镜子，你对它笑，它也会对你笑；你对它哭，它也会对你哭。”如果对生活感恩，你的生活将充满灿烂的阳光；如果一味怨恨，终将一无所获。我们成功时，有千万个理由感恩生活；而失败时，只要一个借口就会表现出忘恩负义。

我想，不论是遭遇失败还是不幸，我们都应该感谢生活。只有这样，失败后，我们才能发现自己的缺点和不足；不幸时，我们还能感受到安慰和温暖。这些就能帮我们找回勇气，战胜困难，并获取前进的强大推动力。我们应像罗斯福总统那样，换一个角度去看待生活中的失败和挫折，永远对生活充满感恩之心，才能时刻保持健康的心态，积极地生活，并能保持完美的人格和不断进取的精神。感恩不仅仅是一种精神慰藉，也不是对现实的逃避，更不是阿Q的精神胜利法。感恩源于我们对生活的热爱和希望，它是我们歌颂生活的一种方式。

把一小块明矾放入混沌的水中，我们发现，水很快就澄清了。如果人人都有一颗感恩的心，就能沉淀许多浮躁和不安，消融许多不满和不幸。感恩能让我们的生活变得更加美好。

Once President Roosevelt's house was broken into and lots of things were stolen. Hearing this, one of Roosevelt's friends wrote to him and advised him not to take it to his heart so much. President Roosevelt wrote back immediately, saying, "Dear friend, thank you for your letter to comfort me. I'm all right now. I think I should thank God. This is because of the following three reasons: firstly, the thief only stole things from me but did not hurt me at all; secondly, the thief has stolen some of my things instead of all my things; thirdly, most luckily for me, it was the man rather than me who became a thief..."

It was quite unlucky for anyone to be stolen from. However, President Roosevelt had such three reasons to be so grateful. This story tells us how we can learn to be grateful in our life.

Being grateful is an important philosophy of life and a great wisdom. It is impossible for anyone to be lucky and successful all the time so long as he lives in the world. We should learn how to face failure or misfortune bravely and generously and to try to deal with it. If so, should we complain about our life and become frustrated and disappointed ever since then or should we be grateful for our life, rise again ourselves after a fall? William Thackeray, a famous British writer, said, "Life is a mirror. When you smile in front of it, it will also smile and so will it when you cry to it."If you are grateful to life, it will bring you shining sunlight. If you always complain about everything, you may own nothing in the end. When we are successful, we can surely have many reasons for being grateful, but we have only one excuse to show ungratefulness if we fail.

I think we should even be grateful to life whenever we are unsuccessful or unlucky. Only by doing this can we find our weakness and shortcomings when we fail. We can also get relief and warmth when we are unlucky. This can help us find our courage to overcome the difficulties we may face, and receive great impetus to move on. We should treat our frustration and misfortune in our life in the other way just as President Roosevelt did. We should be grateful all the time and keep having a healthy attitude to our life forever, keep having perfect characters and enterprising spirit. Being grateful is not only a kind of comfort, not an escape from life and nor thinking of winning in spirit like Ah Q. Being grateful is a way to sing for our life which comes just from our love and hope.

When we put a small piece of alum into muddy water, we can see the alum can soon make the water clear. If each of us has an attitude of being grateful, we'll be able to get rid of impulse, upset, dissatisfaction and misfortune. Being grateful can bring us a better and more beautiful life.

人人都有烦恼

Every Living Person Has Problems

佚名 / Anonymous

坚强的人成功的奥秘是什么？为何他们能熬过艰苦的岁月，而有些人却被困难压倒呢？为何成功属于坚强之人，而失败的却是另一些人？为何那些坚强的人能一飞冲天，而另一些人却身陷困难的泥沼呢？

其实答案很简单，主要在于他们如何面对自己的问题。的确，生活中每个人都会有各自的烦恼。一个不被困难所困扰的人生，只能是一种幻想，就好比是沙漠中的海市蜃楼。现实就是这样，我们必须接受。

每座山都有它的最高点，每个峡谷都有它的最低点。人生的起起落落，一样也有顶峰与低谷，不会有人一生都成功，也不会有人一直都在失败。问题总有一天会结束。随着时间的流逝，所有问题都会迎刃而解。

或许你无法掌控时势，但你可以选择理性地应对。或许你无法选择时运，但你可以选择面对它的方式。比如，遭遇一场严重的经济挫折，究竟如何做才是积极面对呢？酗酒、吸毒甚至自杀，采取一系列逃避方式算得上积极应对吗？不！当然不是，那些消极的应对方式看似能缓解一时的问题，事实上反而会带来更棘手的麻烦。鼓起勇气去解决问题，才是积极应对的方法。人的一生中有许多看似无法解决的难题，当你能够控制自己面对问题时的反应，事实上你已掌控了问题对你的影响。你对问题的态度是非常重要的，起着决定性的作用，因为它可以使人变得脆弱，也可使人变得坚强。它既可使人做得更好，也可以使人痛苦，这全在于你如何面对它。

总而言之，人能够坚强地渡过困难，往往取决于他们选择积极应对困境的态度。难关不会无止境，只要你永不懈怠，坚持到底。历史告诉我们，每个问题都会有终结，没有解决不了的问题。

What is the secret ingredient of tough people that enables them to succeed? Why do they survive the tough times when others are overcome by them? Why do they win when others lose? Why do they soar when others sink?

The answer is very simple. It's all in how they perceive their problems. Yes, every living person has problems. A problem-free life is an illusion—a mirage in the desert. Accept that fact.

Every mountain has a peak. Every valley has its low point. Life has its ups and downs, its peaks and its valleys. No one is up all the time, nor are they down all the time. Problems do end. They are all resolved in time.

You may not be able to control the times, but you can compose your responses. You may not have chosen your tough time, but you can choose how you will react to it. For instance, what is the positive reaction to a terrible financial setback? In this situation would it be the positive reaction to cop out and run away? Escape through alcohol, drug, or suicide? No! Such negative reactions only produce greater problems by promising a temporary "solution"to the pressing problem. The positive solution to a problem may require courage to initiate it. When you control your reaction to the seemingly uncontrollable problem of life, then in fact you do control the problem's effect on you. Your reaction to the problem is the last word! That's the bottom line. What will you let this problem do to you? It can make you tender or tough. It can make you better or bitter. It all depends on you.

In the final analysis, the tough people who survive the tough times do so because they've chosen to react positively to their predicament. Tough times never last, but tough people do. Tough people stick it out. History teaches us that every problem has a lifespan. No problem is permanent.

体味拥有，心满意足

Think More about What You Have

佚名 / Anonymous

专注于我们想得到的，而不是我们所拥有的，这是我见过的一种最具普遍性和破坏性的心理趋向。我们拥有多少，似乎并无太大区别，我们欲望的清单不断扩充，使我们永远不满足。“我实现了这个愿望就会快乐。”一旦这个欲望得到满足，以后还会出现相同的欲求心理。

我们想要这个或那个。如果得不到，就会不断地去想那些没有的东西，总是感到不满足。如果得到了，在新的条件下，我们又产生同样的心理。所以，尽管我们得到了，还是不开心。如果我们一味地渴求新的欲望，将无法找到幸福。

幸运的是，我们想要获得幸福，有这样一种方法：转换我们思考的重心，从想要的转移到拥有的。我们可以试着去想伴侣的可贵品质，而不去希求他该如何与现在不同；可以为自己拥有一份工作充满感激，而不去抱怨薪水太低；可以设想闭门在家的种种乐趣，而不是渴望去夏威夷度假。可以这样去考虑的事物无穷无尽！一旦你意识到自己又陷入这个思维陷阱——“我希望生活不是这样”时，要退后一步，重新思考，深呼吸，想想你所拥有的。这样，感激之情便会油然而生。当你关注的不再是自己想要的，而是所拥有的时候，你最终得到的一定会比想要的更多；如果你关注伴侣的优秀品德，他就会更可爱；如果你对工作充满感激，而不是抱怨，你会做得更好，工作效率更高，薪水也可能提高；如果你在家能自得其乐，而不是等着去夏威夷享受，你会找到更多的乐趣。假设你真的去了夏威夷，往往会更快乐。即使因为某种偶然没能去成，仍然会过得开心。

记住，从现在开始，多想想你拥有的，而不是你想要的。如果你这样做，你的生活就会比以前更美好，那种感受或许是你生命中的第一次，你将会懂得心满意足的含义。

One of the most pervasive and destructive mental tendencies I've seen is that of focusing on what we want instead of what we have. It doesn't seem to make any difference how much we have; we just keep expanding our list of desires, which guarantees we will remain dissatisfied. The mind-set that says "I'll be happy when this desire is fulfilled" is the same mind-set that will repeat itself once that desire is met.

We want this or that. If we don't get what we want, we keep thinking about all that we don't have and we remain dissatisfied. If we do get what we want, we simply recreate the same thinking in our new circumstances. So, despite getting what we want, we still remain unhappy. Happiness can't be found when we are yearning for new desires.

Luckily, there is a way to be happy. It involves changing the emphasis of our thinking from what we want to what we have. Rather than wishing your spouse was different, try thinking about its wonderful qualities. Instead of complaining about your salary, be grateful that you have a job. Rather than wishing you were able to take a vacation to Hawaii, think of how much fun you have had close to home. The list of possibilities is endless! Each time you notice yourself falling into the "I wish life were different" trap, back off and start over. Take a breath and remember all that you have to be grateful. When you focus not on what you want, but on what you have, you end up getting more of what you want anyway. If you focus on the good qualities of your spouse, it'll be more loving. If you are grateful for your job rather than complaining about it, you'll do a better job, be more productive, and probably end up getting a raise anyway. If you focus on ways to enjoy yourself around home rather than waiting to enjoy yourself in Hawaii, you'll end up having more fun. If you ever do get to Hawaii, you'll be in the habit of enjoying yourself. And, if by some chance you don't, you'll have a great life anyway.

Make a note to yourself to start thinking more about what you have than what you want. If you do, your life will start appearing much better than before. For perhaps the first time in your life, you'll know what it means to feel satisfied.

不要害怕失败

Don't Fear Failure

佚名 / Anonymous

许多职业专家将失败鼓吹为“成功的润滑油”。这种说法并不是让你为了获得神秘的胜利，而先将自己推向某个灾难的边缘。这仅仅是那些成功人士对失败的一种认识。他们能够欣然接受失败，并从失败中懂得：无论尝试什么，都是成功的最好机会。

噢，你在学校或爱情上也许遇到过一些小的挫折，但是这样的失败是毫无意义的。乔治·华盛顿大学的社会经济学教授阿米塔伊·埃茨奥尼说：“永远不要害怕，人人都有一次机会，没有谁会一生都失败。”

意识到失败是很容易的事。《当聪明的人失败时》一书的合著者卡罗莱·海厄特说：“通常，失败会伴随着金钱、自尊或身份地位的损失而出现。”至少，失败的结果是得不到你想要的。

《当不幸降临在好人身上时》的作者罗比·哈罗德·库沙尔说，并不是说理智的人应该盼望灾难的降临，但是巨大的挫折往往是痛苦的深刻教训。它“能让你知道自己的长处，了解自己的短处”。库沙尔写道：“经历挫折是成长过程中的重要一课。”

从失败中汲取教训的人才是企业领导青睐的对象。拥有亿万资产的实业家H．罗斯·佩罗特说：“不断的成功会助长自大、自满之情。我想要那些喜欢战场，愿意斗争的人才。”这其中包括犯诚实的错误。H.罗斯·佩罗特又补充说：“失败者本能地避开冒险，即使是面对形势较好的投机机会时也是如此。你从失败中学到的东西，要比从成功中学到的东西多得多。失败仅仅是在寻找新的挑战时所付出的代价。”

如果害怕失败而让你举步维艰，这里有几条有益的建议：

1. 停止使用“失败”一词

有较高成就的人很少提到“失败”二字，因为使用这个沉重的词说明这个人无法再继续发展。他们更喜欢“小麻烦”、“修正方向”等词。

2. 不要因失败而沮丧

当事情进展不顺利时，你是否本能地为自己贴上了“失败者”的标签？你评价自己的语言可以变成一种有力的现实。一次又一次地称自己是位尚未被雇用的售货员，而不应说自己失业了——也就是你在社会生活中的失败——这样说，你就可以认为自己是“拥有选择权”的人。你可以选择参加学习班来培养新的技能，或者勇敢地选择从事另一个行业。

3. 做好准备

规划一个灾难计划来帮助你自己在灾难降临时不会受到影响。问问你自己，会发生的最糟糕的事情是什么？设想一下失去工作或配偶的情形，会让你清晰地考虑现实的选择。你有足够的保险或存款来使你渡过困难时期吗？如果你的老板解雇了你，你的才能会为你带来收入吗？请记住，汉字中“危机”一词的词义包含两方面：“危险”与“机遇”。

4. 学会聪明地失败

休斯敦某大学教授杰克·马斯顿开设了一门课程，该课程被学生们叫做“失败101”。他让他的学生制造没人会买的冰激凌棒模型。马斯顿说：“他们设计成像仓鼠似的热容器和在飓风中放的风筝。”

尽管这些想法都很可笑，可是一旦学生们把失败看做创新而不是失败时，他们会很勇敢地去尝试做任何事情。马斯顿说，在获得成功之前，大多数学生都至少失败了五次，他们学会了不把失败当做最后的结局。“学生们学会了整装待发，再次准备尝试。”

5. 永不言弃

1975年，厄尔利的哈里森堡建筑公司破产了。那时25岁的他向家人借钱维持经营，而并没有宣布破产。他继续做建筑工作，努力掌握管理上的复杂关系。1982年，他厚着脸皮又借了更多的钱来重新开办自己的公司，并于困难时期在银行中留下了良好的口碑。

厄尔利谨慎地扩大了自己新建筑公司的规模。他还去学校学习商业管理课程。1988年，厄尔利的公司被《Inc.》杂志评为世界发展最快的500家企业之一。

厄尔利没有自满，他时常会想起那段艰难的日子。他说：“我不因成功而自满，所以我总在努力发展我的事业。”

Many career experts tout failure as the castor oil of success. The idea isn't to fling yourself into certain disaster in order to be mystically rewarded with triumph. Rather, it's a simple recognition that people who willingly risk failure and learn from loss have the best chance of succeeding at whatever they try.

Oh, you' ve had minor reverses in school or love, but you haven't failed meaningfully. Never fear, says AmitaiEtzioni, professor of socioeconomics at George Washington University,"Everyone gets a chance. No one lives a failure-proof life forever."

Failure is easy to recognize. "It usually involves loss of money, self-esteem or status," says Carole Hyatt, co-author of When Smart People Fail. At the very least, it is simply not getting what you want.

Not that rational people should wish for calamity, says Rabbi Harold Kushner, author of When Bad Things Happen to Good People, But a stiff dose of misfortune is often a painfully effective tutor. It "teaches you something about your strength and acquaints you with your limitations". notes Kushner, "That's an important part of maturity."

People who profit from loss are the kind of foot soldiers business leaders seek, "Continuous success builds arrogance and complacency," says multibillionaire industrialist H. Ross Perot, "I want people who love the battlefield, people willing to go to the war." That includes making honest mistakes. Unsuccessful people, he adds, instinctively avoid risks even when a smart gamble might pay off. "You learn a great deal more from what doesn't work than from what does." Failure, he says, is merely the cost of seeking new challenge.

If the thought of fouling up paralyzes you, here are several helpful suggestions:

1. Stop using the "F" word.

High achievers, rarely refer to "failure," a loaded word suggesting a personal dead end. They prefer "glitch" "bollix" or "course correction."

2. Don't take it personally.

When things go sour, do you instinctively label yourself a loser? The language you use to describe yourself can become a powerful reality. Repeatedly calling yourself an unemployed salesperson not only labels you as out of work—synonymous with failure in our society—it considers yourself someone "with options". Those opinions include taking classes to develop new skills or bravely striking out on another career.

3. Be prepared.

Help insulate yourself by mapping a catastrophe plan. Ask yourself: What is the worst that can happen? Imagining loss of job or spouse can force you to clearly consider practical alternatives. Do you have enough insurance and cash reserves to carry you through a difficult period? Do you have talents that could bring in an income if your employer handed you a pink slip? Keep in mind that the Chinese ideogram for "crisis" consists of the characters for both "danger" and "opportunity."

4. Learn to fail intelligently.

Jack Matson, a University of Houston professor, developed a course his students dubbed "Failure 101". Matson had his class build ice-cream-stick mock-ups of products no one would buy. “They designed hamster hot tubs and kites to fly in hurricanes,” says Matson.

The ideas were ridiculous, but once Matson’s students equated failure with innovation instead of defeat, they felt free to try anything. Since most students had at least five failures before finding their business niche, they learned not to take failure as the last word, says Matson. “They learned to reload and get ready to shoot again.”

5. Never say die.

Early’s Harrisonburg, construction company went belly up in 1975. Then only 25, Early borrowed on his home rather than declare bankruptcy. He continued to work in construction, trying to master the intricacies of management. In 1982, he “got nervy enough” to borrow more to start his own business again, having built a solid reputation with banks for getting through difficult times.

Early expanded his new construction business cautiously. He took college courses in business administration. By 1988, Early’s company made Inc. magazine’s list of the 500 fastest-growing privately owned companies.

Early is not complacent. Memories of hard times haunt him. “I can’t afford to get arrogant about success,” he says, “So I’m always trying to improve my business.”

生活中我们最幸福的时刻

In Life, We Are the Happiest When...

佚名 / Anonymous

一个男人与他的女朋友举行了一场盛大的结婚典礼。

所有的亲朋好友都来参加，分享他们的喜悦，对他们表示祝贺，大家都很愉快。

身着雪白婚纱的新娘楚楚动人，穿着黑色礼服的新郎英俊潇洒。大家看得出来，他们彼此相爱。

婚后数月，妻子提议："我刚在杂志上看到一篇文章，讲的是如何增进夫妻感情。我们各自在纸上罗列出对方的小缺点，然后一起讨论如何解决的办法，会使我们的婚姻生活更融洽。"

丈夫很赞成。于是，他们分头找了个房间，想对方的缺点。那天余下的时间，他们都在想这个问题，同时也把所想的写了下来。

第二天早上，吃早餐时，他们决定谈谈彼此的缺点。

"我先来吧。"妻子说。她拿出单子，上面都写满了，足有三页纸。开始念纸上写的丈夫的小毛病时，她

注意到他的眼角湿润了。

“怎么了？”她问道。“没什么，”丈夫答道，“继续念啊。”

妻子接着念，念完以后，她把单子整齐地放在桌上，两手交叉放在上面。

“现在，该你了。你念完后，我们就来谈谈这些缺点吧。”妻子开心地说道。

丈夫平静地说：“我什么也没写，我觉得你这样已经很完美了，不用为我改变。你很可爱，也很迷人，我不想改变你的任何事情。”

丈夫诚实、深沉的爱与包容，深深地触动了她。她转过头去，哭了起来。

生活中，已经有很多时候，我们都会感到失望、沮丧和厌烦，真的不用再去刻意寻找它们。我们拥有一个充满美丽、光明和希望的美好世界。我们环顾四周，就可以发觉这些美好，那又何必把光阴耗费在寻找不快、失落和烦恼上呢？

A man and his girlfriend were married. It was a large celebration.

All of their friends and family came to see the lovely ceremony and to partake of the festivities and celebrations. All had a wonderful time.

The bride was gorgeous in her white wedding gown and the groom was very dashing in his black tuxedo. Everyone could tell that the love they had for each other was true.

A few months later, the wife came to the husband with a proposal, "I read in a magazine, a while ago, about how we can strengthen our marriage,"she offered, "Each of us will write a list of the things that we find a bit annoying with the other person. Then, we can talk about how we can fix them together and make our lives happier together."

The husband agreed. So each of them went to a separate room in the house and thought of the things that annoyed them about the other. They thought about this question for the rest of the day and wrote down what they came up with.

The next morning, at the breakfast table, they decided that they would go over their lists.

"I'll start,"offered the wife. She took out her list. It had many items on it, enough to fill 3 pages. In fact. As she started reading the list of the little annoyances, she noticed that tears were starting to appear in her husband's eyes.

"What's wrong?"she asked. "Nothing,"the husband replied, "keep reading your list."

The wife continued to read until she had read all three pages to her husband.

She neatly placed her list on the table and folded her hands over the top of it.

"Now, you read your list and then we'll talk about the things on both of our lists."She said happily.

Quietly the husband stated, "I don't have anything on my list. I think that you are perfect the way that you are. I don't want you to change anything for me. You are lovely and wonderful and I wouldn't want to try and change anything about you."

The wife, touched by his honesty and the depth of his love for her and his acceptance of her, turned her head and wept.

In life, there are enough times when we are disappointed, depressed and annoyed. We don't really have to go looking for them. We have a wonderful world that is full of beauty, light and promise. Why waste time in this world looking for the bad, disappointing or annoying when we can look around us, and see the wondrous things before us?

每次只打开一扇门

One Door Every Time

佚名 / Anonymous

20年前，当我们生第一个孩子的时候，我和丈夫约翰就商量好了，我要在家里做全职妈妈，这意味着我们就得只靠他一个人的工资生活了。为了还房贷和学生贷款，我们节衣缩食。我们常以通心粉和奶酪为主食，而且再也没有去看过电影。

我们剪下商家的优惠券，并且买打折的商品。在星期二，廉价旧货店会出售“新”商品；星期三，快过期的肉类和奶类商品会半价出售；星期六，我们会赶在别人之前去买私人摆在门前要出售的商品。但是，对于这一切我早就习惯了，因为我从小就过着缺吃少穿的生活。因此为了摆脱贫困，我早就定下了实际目标，即上大学，拥有牢固的婚姻和一份事业。这些我都做到了，但是，我仍然无法想象为何我的生活会不如意。我的信念更像是希望得到一张安全网，而不能成为我企盼美好生活的理由。

那天的一个电话让我的生活有了转机。“谢莉吗？我是比尔·波特。”我听到电话那端的声音。比尔是一名上门推销的推销员，我上高中的时候，替他送过货。“你愿不愿意再回来为我送货？每周工作几天。”我和约翰商量好，就去给比尔打工了。

你一看到比尔，就会注意他与众不同的外表。他的耳朵特别大，走路时，弯着腰，拖着步子，右手总攥成一个拳头。他说话的速度非常慢。少女时期的我不好意思提起这些事情，但再次为他工作时，我问起了这个问题。

"比尔，你患有多发性硬化这类疾病吗？"我问。"我患有脑瘫。"他如实地回答。我想，他知道我谈及这个问题会很紧张。"你怎么会得这种病，它会恶化吗？""我出生时，医生的钳子伤到了我的大脑。我的病永远都不会恶化，但也不会好转。然而，这并不影响我决心要做的事情。"

比尔的乐观使我很吃惊，特别是这和我的悲观情绪形成了鲜明对比。他感激他的父母，因为是他们教导他要有坚定的信念。他们努力培养他，使他上公立学校，毕业后，父亲对他说："去找工作吧。"这不能说他的父亲苛刻，而恰恰说明他们不想娇惯儿子。他们坚持比尔可以做任何他想做的事情，只要他有决心，他们绝不会让他放弃。比尔获得了沃特金集团公司的一次面试机会，这个公司的推销员要上门推销家用药物和香料。比尔对面试官说："我天生就会推销，任何东西，只要我信任它，我就可以推销出去。您不妨给我个机会，让我试试看。"

这位面试官给了他一份工作——不过，是试用。他敲响了一家又一家的门，一次又一次地被拒绝，后来，开始有人买比尔的东西。比尔每天沿着他的销售路线工作八个小时，有时时间会更长，这样，他成为公司整个西北地区的顶级销售人员。当然，这很不容易，每天早晨4点45分，闹钟就会把他叫醒，而他要坐7点20分开往市区的公交车。比尔需要充足的准备时间，他不想匆忙地穿衣。"外表很重要。"他说。每天早晨，他都穿干净的袜子，熨得平平整整的裤子，还有白色的衬衫。他不会扣袖口上的扣子，鞋带也松松地系上，把领带放在手提包里。在换乘车站附近有一家旅馆，那里的几个朋友会帮他扣上袖口上的扣子，系好鞋带，打好领带。然后，他就走上大街挨家挨户地推销。他对自己说："下一个客户肯定会说'是'的。"更重要的是，比尔相信，他们最终都会同意购买他的商品的。

后来，我又有了几个孩子，但我继续为比尔打工。约翰的工资也长了，可我们继续过着节衣缩食的生活。这已经成为一个强迫性的习惯，我仍然为将来的生活担忧，我的信条依然是要为将来买意外保险，而不是积极地应对目前的生活。而比尔坚持自己的信仰，每天早晨起来都对生活充满最美好的希望。我会像比尔一样乐观地生活吗？丈夫也因为我感到很沮丧。一个周末，约翰想去看电影，他说："我们可以赶得上7点钟的那场。""亲爱的，我们为什么不白天去看呢？"我问，"那样会便宜些。""但是，我们买得起电影票。"我知道约翰是对的，但我总是为钱和将来担忧。这种担忧从孩提时就产生了，根深蒂固，我一直都无法摆脱它的束缚。

冬季的一天，天气预报说波特兰会有大风暴，比尔当然很高兴。"这样的天气对一名上门推销员是非常有利的，"他说，"因为人们都待在家里。"所以他把商品捆起来，挨家挨户地去推销，一直工作到完成销售任务。这时，由于天气原因造成的糟糕路况，导致公交车停运了。他不得不搭便车回家，下车后，他却发现家门前那条陡峭的车道太滑了，他多次摔倒又再次爬起，最终手脚并用地爬回了家。然而，他心里特别高兴，为那天圆满的工作而高兴。第二天上午，他把发生的事告诉了我。也许是由于长时间为比尔工作，受到他乐观精神的影响，我不再为将来的生活发愁了，而是开始享受生活。

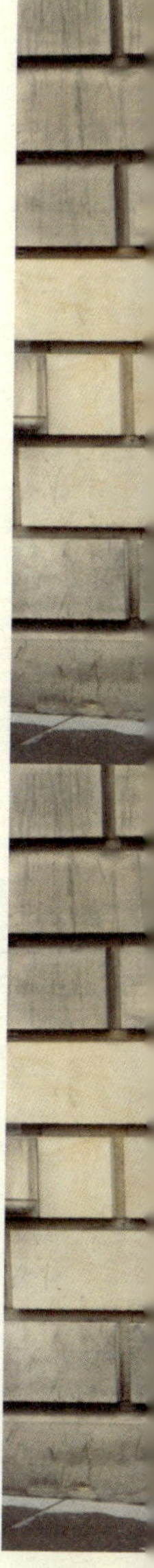

我已经为比尔工作了20年。有时，以前的焦虑感还会影响我，每当这时，我就会想起我的朋友比尔在他家门前结满冰的车道上爬行的情景，我听到他说：“谢莉，生活中没有阻碍，只有挑战。”当我向他学习时，我就会放松，就会感到自由。是的，比尔最终让我希望上帝在赐予我们机会时，每次只开一道门。现在，我们家去看电影时都买全价的电影票，而且，我们还舍得花钱买爆米花了。

When my husband, John, and I had our first child 20 years ago, we agreed I'd be a stay-at-home mom. That meant we'd have to make do on a single income. We scrimped and saved so we could keep with the mortgage and our student loans. We ate a lot of macaroni and cheese dinners. We even didn't go to the movies anymore.

I clipped coupons and tracked down sales. Tuesday was when the thrift stores put out their "new"merchandise. Wednesday was when the meat and dairy section goods were marked at half price just prior to their expiration date. Saturday morning meant getting to the garage sales before anyone else. But none of this was unfamiliar. I grew up wanting. So I had set my sights on realistic goals that would get me out of poverty: a college education, a solid marriage and a career. I'd had done it all, yet I still couldn't imagine things would never go right for me. My faith felt more like a safety net than a reason to have hope for a better life.

Things took a turn one day when I got a phone call. "Shelly? This is Bill Porter,"the voice on the end of the line said. Bill was a door-to-door salesman I'd delivered packages for in high school. "Would you be interested in coming back a couple of days a week to fill orders for me?"I talked about it with John, and then went to work for Bill.

The first thing you notice about Bill is his unusual appearance. His ears are very large. He walks—or rather, shuffles—stooped over. His right hand is balled up almost into a fist. And he takes a long time to get his words out. When I was a teen I was too shy to ask about it. But one day after I started to work for him again

I posed the question.

"Bill, do you have MS or something like that?"I asked. "I have cerebral palsy,"he answered matter-of-factly. I think he knew I was nervous talking about it. "But... what does that mean? How did you get it? Will it get worse? " "The doctor's forceps damaged my brain at my birth. My condition will never get any worse. But it won't get any better, either. It doesn't stop me from accomplishing whatever I set my mind to."

Bill's optimism amazed me, especially in contrast to my own tendency toward pessimism. He gave credits to his parents, who taught him a strong faith. They fought to get him into public school; after he graduated, his father told him, "Get a job."He wasn't being harsh. It's just that they'd never coddled Bill; instead, they had always insisted he could do anything he set his mind to and they never let him give up. Bill got an interview with Watkins Incorporated, a company whose salesmen peddle home remedies and spices door to door. Bill told the director, "Selling is in my blood. It almost doesn't matter what the product is, as long as I believe in it. Give me a chance and you'll see."

The director gave Bill a job on a trial basis. He knocked on door after door and heard no after no. Then Bill started making sales. He walked his route eight hours a day, or more, and became the company's top salesman in the entire Northwest. It wasn't easy. Every morning, Bill's alarm went off at 4:45 a.m. His bus downtown left at 7:20 a.m. Bill needed all that time because he doesn't like to dress in a rush. "Appearance is essential,"he said. Each morning he put on clean socks, pressed trousers and fresh white shirt. He would leave his cuffs unbuttoned, his wingtips loosely tied, and his tie in the briefcase. Some friends at a hotel near where he made a bus transfer attended to those loose ends. Bill would hit the streets, knocking on every single door, telling himself, "The next customer will say yes."The key is, Bill believes they'll all say yes eventually.

I kept working for Bill even after I had a few more children. John was making more money, but I continued to scrimp and save. Honestly, it had become a compulsion. I still went through life with a sense of foreboding. Faith was still an insurance policy against disaster rather than a way to meet life head-on. Bill used his faith every day, getting out of bed and expecting the best. Would I ever look at life that way? Even my husband was frustrated with me. One weekend John wanted to go to a movie. "We can catch the seven o'clock show." "Honey, can't we go to the matinee?"I asked, "It's cheaper." "We can afford it."He was right, but I couldn't stop worrying about money and the future. It all stemmed from my childhood, and I'd never be able to overcome that.

One winter day a storm was forecast for Portland. Of course to Bill the weather report was good news. "Perfect for a door-to-door salesman,"he said, "Everyone's at home!"So he bundled up and made his rounds until he had made his quota. But then, the buses had stopped running because the roads were so bad. He had to hitchhike home, only to discover the steep driveway leading to his front door was a sheet of ice. He tried to get up it again and again, but kept falling down. Finally he got down on his hands and knees and crawled to the front door thoroughly satisfied with his day's work. He told me about it the next morning. It was as if the cumulative affect of working with Bill and his optimism sank in. I wanted to stop worrying about life and start enjoying it.

It's been 20 years now that I've worked for Bill. Once in a while those old worries start in on me. It is then I think about my friend Bill crawling up his icy driveway. I hear him saying, "There are no obstacles, Shelly. Only challenges."When I follow his example, I'm able to let go and feel free. Yes, Bill Porter's finally got me looking forward to the opportunities God opens for us, one door at a time. And these days when my family goes to the movies we see the full-priced show and splurge on popcorn.

输赢不是争吵出来的

[美]戴尔·卡耐基 / Dale Carnegie

You Can't Win an Argument

多年前，帕特里克·欧·海瑞参加了我的成人教育班。帕特文化水平不高，却很喜欢和人争论。他曾做过司机，之所以来向我求助，是因为他推销卡车没能成功。这是由一个小问题引发的——他总是不断地与客户争论而触怒他们。一旦对方对他销售的汽车稍有不满，帕特便会喋喋不休，没完没了。那段时期，帕特赢了不少场争论。正如他后来对我所说的那样：“我常常走出办公室便自言自语道：‘我好好地教训了他。’我确实教训了他，可我没有卖出想卖的车。”

我首先需要解决的不是教帕特如何去说话，最紧迫的是，我要帮他克制自己，避免争吵。

如今，欧·海瑞已经是纽约怀特汽车公司的销售明星。

他是如何做到的呢？让我们听听他自己是怎么说的：“如果我现在向某个客户推销，而他说：‘什么？怀特汽车？怀特汽车一点儿也不好。就算你白给

我一辆，我也不会要的。我想买一辆胡佛牌汽车。’我就会说：‘胡佛牌汽车确实是好汽车，如果你选择了那个牌子，肯定是不会错的。胡佛汽车是由知名厂家生产的，他们的销售人员也很出色。’”

“这样，他就没什么可说的了。根本没有争吵的空间。如果他说那个是最好的品牌，我随即表示认可，他就无言以对了。当我认同时，他不可能整个下午都谈论胡佛汽车的优点。当我们绕开话题时，我就会开始谈论怀特汽车的好处。”

“要是在以前，只要他一说出刚才那样的话，我就会变得暴跳如雷，一味地挑剔胡佛汽车的缺点。我越是争吵，就会越有利于胡佛汽车；而客户呢，他越是争吵，就越容易买我竞争对手的车。”

“现在回首往事，我真不知自己过去是如何推销货物的。我把自己的生命浪费在争吵之中。我现在学会了闭住嘴巴，并且从中受益匪浅。”

就像聪明的富兰克林所言："假如你喜欢喋喋不休，争强好胜，那么你也许偶尔会赢。可是这种胜利没有什么实际意义，因为你永远获得不了对方的好感。"

所以，好好地反省一下自己。理论上虚假的胜利和一个人发自内心的好感，你会选择哪一种呢？你不可能同时拥有。

因为一笔9000美元的重要账目，个人所得税顾问弗雷德里克·佩森与一名政府税务稽查员争论了将近一个小时。佩森声称，这9000美元是呆账，根本不可能收上来，所以不应该征收所得税。而那位顽固的稽查员说："不可能，一定要征收。"

佩森在课堂上对学生们讲述道："那位稽查员是一个骄傲、自大、顽固的人。解释根本没有作用。事实上，我们越是争吵，他就越顽固。所以，我就不再与他争吵，试着转变话题，表示理解他的工作。

“我说：‘与你处理的那些极其重要且困难的事相比，这件事情根本不值一提。我只是自学了税务，而且仅仅局限于书本，而你的税务知识全凭实践而来。说实话，我十分羡慕你的工作，它可以教会我很多东西。’”

“哦。”那位稽查员直起身跟我谈了很久。关于他的工作——他告诉了我许多工作中的技巧。他的语气变得缓和了许多，后来还谈起了自己的孩子。临走时，他告诉我，他会仔细考虑一下我的问题，并在几天内给我答复。

“三天后，我在办公室里接到了他的电话。他通知我，那笔所得税不征收了。”

人性中最常见的弱点在这位稽查员的身上得到了很好的验证。他想得到被重视的感觉。所以，当佩森先生与他争吵时，他固执地展示权威来找到被重视的感觉。然而，一旦重视感得到满足，争吵停止，便会展现出他宽容、温和的一面。

Years ago Patrick J.O'Haire Joined one of my classes. He had little education, and how he loved a scrap! He had once been a chauffeur, and he came to me because he had been trying, without much success, to sell trucks. A little questioning brought out the fact that he was continually scrapping with and antagonizing the very people he was trying to do business with, if a prospect said anything derogatory about the trucks he was selling, Pat saw red and was right at the customer's throat. Pat won a lot of arguments in those days. As he said to me afterward, "I often walked out of an office saying, 'I told that bird something.'Sure I had told him something, but I hadn't sold him anything."

My first problem was not to teach Patrick J. O'Haire to talk. My immediate task was to train him to refrain from talking and to avoid verbal fights.

Mr. O'Haire became one of the star salesmen for the White Motor Company in New York.

How did he do it? Here is his story in his own words, "If I walk into a buyer's office now and he says, 'What? A White truck? They're no good! I wouldn't take one if you gave it to me. I'm going to buy the Whose-It truck.'I say, 'The Whose-It is a good truck. If you buy the Whose-It, you'll never make a mistake. The Whose-Its are made by a fine company and sold by good people.'

"He is speechless then. There is no room for an argument. If he says the Whose-It is best and I say sure it is, he has to stop. He can't keep on all afternoon saying, 'It's the best'when I'm agreeing with him. We then get off the subject of Whose-It and I begin to talk about the good points of the White truck.

"There was a time when a remark like his first one would have made me see scarlet and red and orange. I would start arguing against the Whose-It; and the more I argued against it, the more my prospect argued in favor of it; and the more he argued, the more he sold himself on my competitor's product.

"As I look back now I wonder how I was ever able to sell anything. I lost years of my life in scrapping and arguing. I keep my mouth shut now. It pays."

As wise old Ben Franklin used to say: "If you argue and rankle and contradict, you may achieve a victory sometimes; but it will be an empty victory because you will never get your opponent's good will."

So figure it out for yourself. Which would you rather have, an academic, theatrical victory or a person's good will? You can seldom have both.

Frederick S. Parsons, an income tax consultant, had been disputing and wrangling for an hour with a goverment tax inspector. An item of nine thousand dollars was at stake. Mr. Parsons claimed that this nine thousand dollars was in reality a bad debt, that it would never be collected, that it ought not to be taxed. "Bad debt.myeye!"retorted the inspector, "It must be taxed. "

"This inspector was cold, arrogant and stubborn,"Mr. Parsons said as he told the story to the class, "Reason was wasted and so were facts... The longer we argued, the more stubborn he became. So I decided to avoid argument, change the subject, and give him appreciation.

"I said, 'I suppose this is a very petty matter in comparison with the really important and difficult decisions you're required to make. I've made a study of taxation myself. But I've had to get my knowledge from books. You are getting yours from the firing line of experience. I sometime wish I had a job like yours. It would teach me a lot.' I meant every word I said."

"Well. "The inspector straightened up in his chair, leaned back, and talked for a long time about his work, telling me of the clever frauds he had uncovered. His tone gradually became friendly, and presently he was telling me about his children. As he left, he advised me that he would consider my problem further and give me his decision in a few days.

"He called at my office three days later and informed me that he had decided to leave the tax return exactly as it was filed."

This tax inspector was demonstrating one of the most common of human frailties. He wanted a feeling of importance; and as long as Mr. Parsons argued with him, he got his feeling of importance by loudly asserting his authority. But as soon as his importance was admitted and the argument stopped and he was permitted to expand his ego, he became a sympathetic and kindly human being.

成为一个健谈者

An Easy Way to Become a Good Conversationalist

[美] 戴尔·卡耐基 / Dale Carnegie

前段时间，我去参加了一次桥牌聚会。可我不会打桥牌，刚好有一位女士也不会打，我们便一起聊天。当她得知我曾在汤姆森先生从事广播事业之前，为了帮助汤姆森准备一些有关旅行栏目的演讲内容而特意到欧洲各地去旅行时，便对我说：“啊！卡耐基先生，您能不能把您游览过的名胜古迹或美景讲给我听呢？”

我们刚坐到沙发上，她便告诉我，她和她的丈夫前不久刚从非洲旅行回来。

我说：“非洲！那可是一个有趣的地方！我一直梦想着能到那片土地去看看，可我只是在阿尔及尔待过24小时，便再没有去过非洲其他地方。快给我讲讲吧，你真的去过那个伟大的地方吗？是吗？多么幸运啊！我真是太羡慕你了！请告诉我一些有关非洲的情形吧！”

随后，她绘声绘色地讲了整整45分钟。她根本没再问我到过欧洲哪些地方和在异地的所见所闻。事实上，她根本不想听我讲旅行的事情，她唯一需要的不过是一个专注的倾听者，好让她借此机会讲述自己曾经到过的地方。

在日常生活中，这位女士不同寻常吗？不，很多人都是这样的。

比如，在纽约一位出版商的晚宴上，我曾经遇到了一位声名显赫的植物学家。我以前从未与植物学家交谈过，只是觉得他有极强的个人魅力。我毕恭毕敬地坐在椅子上倾听，他便滔滔不绝地介绍大麻、改良植物新品种的实验，以及布置室内花园等（他还向我讲述了许多有关廉价马铃薯的惊人事实）。我家里也有一个小型的室内花园，他耐心而友好地替我解决了我所遇到的一些疑惑。

就像我所说的，我们是在宴会上，其他十几位客人也一定在场。然而，我忽略了所有礼节上的规矩，把那些客人全部放在一边，与这位植物学家谈了几个小时。

午夜时分，我向大家告辞后，便离开了。这位植物学家找到宴会主人，对我大加赞赏，他说我是“最富激励性的人”，我有多好多好。最后，还说我是个“最有趣的健谈者”。

一个有趣的健谈者？为什么？我几乎没说什么话。如果我不选择改变话题的话，就算我想说，我也说不出什么来，因为我对植物学方面知识的了解少得可怜，就像对企鹅的解剖一样一窍不通。然而，我做了这样一件事：我专注地倾听对方讲话。而我这样做，是因为我真的对话题产生了兴趣。他也感觉到这一点，而这一点显然让他很开心。专注地倾听他人讲话，就是对他人最好的尊敬。

所以，如果你想成为一个健谈者，那么就要做一个善于倾听的人。如果你想使别人对你产生兴趣，你首先要对别人产生兴趣。提出一些他人喜欢回答的问题，激励他们谈自己，谈他们的成就。

千万不要忘记，对面那个正在与你交谈的人，对于他自身的需求，以及自身问题的关注程度，远比对你的兴趣高一百倍。一个人对脖子上一颗小痣的关注程度，要远远超过对非洲四十次地震的关注。下次你跟别人谈话的时候想想这个，做一个好的聆听者，激励对方多谈论自己。

Some time ago, I attended a bridge party. I don't play bridge and there was a woman there who didn't play bridge either. She had discovered that I had once been Lowell Thomas' manager before he went on the radio and that I had traveled in Europe a great deal while helping him prepare the illustrated travel talks he was then delivering. So she said: "Oh, Mr. Carnegie, I do want you to tell me about all the wonderful places you have visited and the sights you have seen."

As we sat down on the sofa, she remarked that she and her husband had recently returned from a trip to Africa.

"Africa!"I exclaimed, "How interesting! I've always wanted to see Africa, but I never got there except for a twenty-four-hour stay once in Algiers. Tell me, did you visit the big-game country? Yes? How fortunate. I envy you. Do tell me about Africa."

That kept her talking for forty-five minutes. She never again asked me where I had been or what I had seen. She didn't want to hear me talk about my travels. All she wanted was an interested listener, So she could expand her ego and tell about where she had been.

Was she unusual? No. Many people are like that.

For example, I met a distinguished botanist at a dinner party given by a New York book publisher. I had never talked with a botanist before, and I found him fascinating. I literally sat on the edge of my chair and listened while he spoke of exotic plants and experiments in developing new forms of plant life and indoor gardens (and even told me astonishing facts about the humble potato). I had a small indoor garden of my own, and he was good enough to tell me how to solve some of my problems.

As I said, we were at a dinner party. There must have been a dozen other guests,but I violated all the canons of courtesy, ignored everyone else, and talked for hours to the botanist.

Midnight came, I said good night to everyone and departed. The botanist then turned to our host and paid me several flattering compliments. I was "most stimulating". I was this and I was that, and he ended by saying I was a "most interesting conversationalist".

An interesting conversationalist? Why, I had said hardly anything at all. I couldn't have said anything if I had wanted to without changing the subject, for I didn't know any more about botany than I knew about the anatomy of a penguin. But I had done this: I had listened intently. I had listened because I was genuinely interested. And he felt it. Naturally that pleased him. That kind of listening is one of the highest compliments we can pay anyone.

So if you aspire to be a good conversationalist, be an attentive listener. To be interesting, be interested. Ask questions that other persons will enjoy answering. Encourage them to talk about themselves and their accomplishments.

Remember that the people you are talking to are a hundred times more interested in themselves and their wants and problems than they are in you and your problems. A boil on one's neck interests one more than forty earthquakes in Africa. Think of that the next time you start a conversation. Be a good listener. Encourage others to talk about themselves.

多一小时的清醒

How to Add One Hour a Day to your Waking Life

我为什么要在一本谈论排忧的书里写有关避免疲劳的问题呢？原因很简单，因为疲劳常常会带来烦恼，至少会使你容易感到烦恼。任何一个医科学生都会告诉你，疲劳会降低身体对普通感冒和其他上百种疾病的抵抗力。任何一位心理学家都会告诉你，疲劳会降低你对恐惧和烦闷的抵抗力。所以，避免疲劳有助于避免忧虑。

我刚才说“可以避免忧虑”吗？这句话表达得缺少力度。芝加哥大学实验心理学实验室主任埃德蒙·雅各布解释得更明确一些。他写了两本有关放松的书——《消除紧张情绪》和《放松紧张情绪》。多年来，他一直在临床实践中运用放松紧张情绪的方法，并进行了相关方面的研究。他声称，任何精神或是情绪的紧张状态“在完全放松的状态下就会消失”。换句话说，如果你处于放松状态，就不会再忧虑了。

所以，为了避免疲劳和忧虑，第一条规则就是：经常休息，在你感到疲倦之前休息。

这一条为什么很重要呢？因为疲劳的累积速度快得惊人。美国陆军经过反复试验得出：受过多年军事训练的年轻人，如果他们丢下包，每小时休息10分钟的话，他们的行军速度会很快，并能持续很长时间。所以，陆军部队强制他们要这样做。

H T A O H

你的心脏与美国陆军士兵的心脏一样健康。心脏每天为你身体提供的血液，你的心脏24小时内所提供的能量足以把20吨煤铲到3英尺高的月台上。心脏承受如此大的工作量，要持续五七十年甚至九十年，心脏是如何承受的呢？哈佛医院的华特·坎农博士解释说："大多数人都认为心脏是在一直不停地工作。事实上，心脏每收缩一次，都会停止一段时间，再以每分钟70次的速度跳动。24小时中，心脏的实际工作时间仅有9小时，每天的休息时间总计长达15小时。"

体力劳动者如果每天有足够的时间休息，那么，他就可以干更多的活。弗雷德里克·泰勒在伯利恒钢铁公司担任科学管理工程师期间，通过观察发现：每个工人每天往货车上搬运12.5吨生铁，到了中午，他就筋疲力尽了。弗雷德里克·泰勒对导致工人疲劳的因素作了一次科学研究。他认为，这些工人每天不应只装运12.5吨生铁，而是47吨。他认为，工人们应该创造的工作

D T Y W L

量至少是现在的四倍。不过，我们要证明一下。

泰勒挑选了施密特先生，要求他按秒表的时间工作。施密特让一个人拿着表站在他身边："现在开始搬运生铁，走……现在坐下来，休息一会儿……现在走……现在休息。"

发生了什么呢？普通工人每天只搬运12.5吨生铁，而施密特一天搬运了47吨。而且，他在伯利恒钢铁公司工作的三年里，工作能力并未下降过。施密特能够做到这样，是因为他在感到劳累之前就休息了。他每工作26分钟，就要休息34分钟。他的休息时间要长过工作时间，但工作量是其他人的四倍！这是传言吗？不是，你可以阅读一下弗雷德里克·泰勒的《科学管理法则》。

让我再重复一遍：按照陆军的方法去做——频繁的休息；按照心脏的跳动规律去做——在感到疲劳之前就休息。这样，你每天的清醒时间就会增加一小时。

Why am I writing a chapter on preventing fatigue in a book on preventing worry? That is simple: because fatigue often produces worry, or, at least, it makes you susceptible to worry. Any medical student will tell you that fatigue lowers physical resistance to the common cold and hundreds of other diseases and any psychiatrist will tell you that fatigue also lowers your resistance to the emotions of fear and worry. So preventing fatigue tends to prevent worry.

Did I say "tends to prevent worry"? That is putting it mildly. Dr. Edmund Jacobson goes much further. Dr. Jacobson has written two books on relaxation: Progressive Relaxation and You Must Relax, and as director of the University of Chicago Laboratory for Clinical Physiology, he has spent years conducting investigations in using relaxation as a method in medical practice. He declares that any nervous or emotional state "fails to exist in the presence of complete relaxation". That is another way of saying: You cannot continue to worry if you relax.

So, to prevent fatigue and worry, the first rule is: Rest often. Rest before you get tired.

Why is that so important? Because fatigue accumulate with astonishing rapidity. The United States Army has discovered by repeated tests that even young men—men toughened by years of Army training—can march better, and hold up longer, if they throw down their packs and rest ten minutes out of every hour. So the Army forces them to do just that.

Your heart is just as smart as the U. S. Army. Your heart pumps enough blood through your body every day to fill a railway tank car. It exerts enough energy every twenty-four hours to shovel twenty tons of coal on to a platform three feet high. It does this incredible amount of work for fifty, seventy, or maybe ninety years. How can it stand it? Dr. Walter B. Cannon, of the Harvard Medical School, explains it. He says, "Most people have the idea that the heart is working all the time. As a matter of fact, there is a definite rest period after each contraction. When beating at a moderate rate of seventy pulses per minute, the heart is actually working only nine hours out of the twenty-four. In the aggregate its rest periods total a full fifteen hours per day."

A physical worker can do more work if he takes more time out for rest. Frederick Taylor demonstrated that while working as a scientific management engineer with the Bethlehem Steel Company. He observed that labouring men were loading approximately 12 1/2 tons of pig-iron per man each day on freight cars and that they were exhausted at noon. He made a scientific study of all the fatigue factors involved,and declared that these men should be loading not 12 1/2 tons of pig-iron per day, but forty-seven tons per day! He figured that they ought to do almost four times as much as they were doing, and not be exhausted. But prove it!

Taylor selected a Mr. Schmidt who was required to work by the stop-watch. Schmidt was told by the man who stood over him with a watch: "Now pick up a 'pig'and walk... now sit down and rest... now walk... now rest."

What happened? Schmidt carried forty-seven tons of pig-iron each day while the other men carried only 12.5 tons per man. And he practically never failed to work at this pace during the three years that Frederick Taylor was at Bethlehem. Schmidt was able to do this because he rested before he got tired. He worked approximately 26 minutes out of the hour and rested 34 minutes. He rested more than he worked—yet he did almost four times as much work as the others!Is this mere hearsay? No, you can read the record yourself in Principles of Scientific Management by Frederick Winslow Taylor.

Let me repeat: do what the Army does—take frequent rests. Do what your heart does—rest before you get tired, and you will add one hour a day to your waking life.

Finding What You Do not Seek

探寻未知也是一种快乐

[美]奥里森·马登 / Orison Marden

一天，在詹姆士·罗斯查尔德爵士家的宴会上，法国著名画家欧仁·德拉克罗瓦当场透露：在过去的一段时间里，他一直发愁为正在创作中的画寻找一位乞丐模特。当他的目光停留在爵士脸上时，灵感突然闪现在脑中——他梦寐以求的模特就在眼前。作为一名忠实的艺术爱好者，罗斯查尔德高兴地答应扮演一名乞丐。第二天，在德拉克罗瓦的画室里，他将一件束腰外衣围在爵士肩上，让爵士手握一根短棍，并摆出一个造型，如同正在一座古罗马神庙前的阶梯上休息一样。德拉克罗瓦离开画室后，他最得意的一名学生进来看到了罗斯查尔德的乞丐造型。年轻人自然而然地认为这个乞丐是刚刚被带进画室，便带着同情的表情一声不吭地将一些钱塞在他手里。罗斯查尔德只是道了声谢，便把钱放进兜里，那个学生走出了画室。后来，罗斯查尔德从画家那里得知，那个年轻人很有绘画天分，只是缺乏处世经验。

没过多久，那个年轻人便收到了一封信。信中大意是，因为他的善良本性，将钱给了一个他认为是乞丐的人，而作为答谢，他将得到一万法郎，可以随时到罗斯查尔德的办公室领取。

这件事充分地说明了艺术的魅力，即使富有的人也不例外——画家的灵感，假扮的乞丐，以及一个可敬学生的善举。

德国教育家威廉·冯·洪堡说过：“尤其值得注意的是，当我们不过度担忧自己是否快乐，而是全身心地严格履行职责时，快乐自然就会来临。”

快乐的感觉不正像波光粼粼的水流吗？英国前首相格莱斯顿曾说：“我最大的快乐是在工作中得到的。我从小就养成了勤奋的习惯，并因此受益匪浅。年轻人很容易认为休息就是停止一切努力，可我觉得最佳的休息就是转变为另一种形式的努力。如果看书、学习太多而感到头昏脑涨，就出去晒一下温暖的阳光，呼吸一下新鲜的空气，让身心得到彻底的放松。大脑不久就会恢复平静并得到休息。天性中的努力成分是永不枯竭的，甚至在我们睡觉的时候，心脏也还在不停地跳动着。我试着将自己的生活方式顺应天性，并在劳动中尽力模仿；而最终的结果是甜美的睡眠、健康的消化能力，以及旺盛的精力。我所得到的这些皆源于勤奋的酬劳。”

只有那些把精力集中到一些目标而不是自身幸福的人，才能获得真正的快乐。“最美好、最显著的快乐是同他人共同分享快乐。”法国教育家拉·布吕耶尔评价道。

美国小说家霍桑也曾说过，相互分享的快乐才是内心所有快乐的巅峰。

从前有一个国王，他十分溺爱自己的小儿子，并想尽办法让小儿子开心。因此，国王买来小马给他骑，建造漂亮的房子让他住，当然少不了图画、书、玩具、老师、伙伴以及一切用钱能买到或没法做到的事情。虽然小王子什么都有，可他还是闷闷不乐。无论走到哪里，他总是一副愁眉苦脸的样子，并一直期待拥有他所没有的东西。直到一位魔术师来到宫廷才改变了一切。魔术师看到愁容满面的小男孩后，便对国王说：“只要我告诉你儿子一个秘密，我就能让他快乐起来，将他的苦脸变为笑脸，可你必须为这个秘密给我一大笔钱。”

“好吧，”国王说，“不管你要什么，我都会答应的。”小男孩被带到一个单独的房间，魔术师用一个白色的东西在一张纸上写了些字，并递给小男孩一支蜡烛，叫他点燃后，把纸放在蜡烛的上方，然后看可以读到什么。吩咐完了后，魔术师就走出了屋子。小男孩按照魔术师的话去做，这时，白色的字母变成了美丽的蓝色，并组成了这样一句话：“每天做一件好事。”王子接受了这个建议，成为王国里最快乐的人。

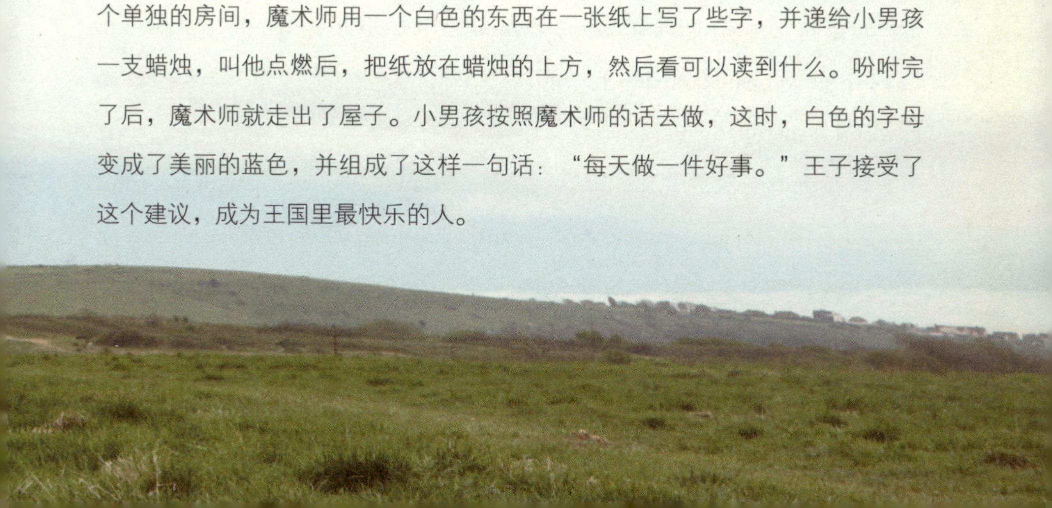

Dining one day with Baron James Rothschild, Eugene Delacroix, the famous French artist, confessed that, during some time past, he had vainly sought for a head to serve as a model for that of a beggar in a picture which he was painting; and that, as he gazed at his host's features, the idea suddenly occurred to him that the very head he desired was before him. Rothschild, being a great lover of art, readily consented to sit as the beggar. The next day, at the studio, Delacroix placed a tunic around the baron's shoulders, put a stoutstaff in his hand, and made him pose as if he were resting on the steps of an ancient Roman temple. In this attitude he was found by one of the artist's favorite pupils, in a brief absence of the master from the room. The youth naturally concluded that the beggar had just been brought in, and with a sympathetic look quietly slipped a piece of money into his hand. Rothschild thanked him simply, pocketed the money, and the student passed out. Rothschild then inquired of the master, and found that the young man had talent, but very slender means.

Soon after, the youth received a letter stating that charity bears interest, and that the accumulated interest on the amount he had given to one he supposed to be a beggar was represented by the sum of ten thousand francs, which was awaiting his claim at the Rothschild office.

This illustrates well the art to cheerful amusement even if one has great business cares—the entertainment of the artist, the personation of a beggar, and an act of beneficence toward a worthy student.

It was said by Wilhelm von Humboldt, that "it is worthy of special remark that when we are not too anxious about happiness and unhappiness, but devote ourselves to the strict and unsparing performance of duty, then happiness comes of itself."

Are not buoyant spirits like water sparkling when it runs? "I have found my greatest happiness in labor,"said Gladstone, "I early formed a habit of industry, and it has been its own reward. The young are apt to think that rest means a cessation from all effort, but I have found the most perfect rest in changing effort. If brain-weary over books and study, go out into the blessed sunlight and the pure air, and give heartfelt exercise to the body. The brain will soon become calm and rested. The efforts of nature are ceaseless. Even in our sleep the heart throbs on. I try to live close to nature, and to imitate her in my labors. The compensation is sound sleep, a wholesome digestion, and powers that are kept at their best; and this, I take it, is the chief reward of industry."

Those only are happy who have their minds fixed on some object other than their own happiness. "The most delicate, the most sensible of all pleasures,"says La Bruyre, "consists in promoting the pleasures of others."

And Hawthorne has said that the inward pleasure of imparting pleasure is the choicest of all.

There was once a king who loved his little boy very much, and took a great deal of pains to please him. So he gave him a pony to ride, beautiful rooms to live in, pictures, books, toys without number, teachers, companions, and everything that money could buy or ingenuity devise; but for all this, the young prince was unhappy. He wore a frown wherever he went, and was always wishing for something he did not have. At length a magician came to the court. He saw the scowl on the boy's face, and said to the king: "I can make your son happy, and turn his frowns into smiles, but you must pay me a great price for telling him this secret."

"All right,"said the king, "whatever you ask I will give."The magician took the boy into a private room. He wrote something with a white substance on a piece of paper. He gave the boy a candle, and told him to light it and hold it under the paper, and then see what he could read. Then the magician went away. The boy did as he had been told, and the white letters turned into a beautiful blue. They formed these words: "Do a kindness to some one every day."The prince followed the advice, and became the happiest boy in the realm.